To my husband, Wally,
for his unwavering love and support, and
to my best friend, Paula,
for never allowing me to give up

SNAP

CALL ME tUESDAY

LEIGH BYRNE

BASED ON A tRUE StORY

AUTHOR'S NOTE

The following is based on a true story. Although the accounts of abuse described herein have been diligently rendered to the best of my recollections, the names, locations and certain identifying details have been fictionalized. Timelines are not exact, and the conversations have been recreated to convey the true meaning of what was said. This story is mine and mine alone, as seen through my eyes.

ISBN: 1463690029
ISBN 13: 9781463690021
Library of Congress Control Number: 2011961407
CreateSpace Independent Publishing Platform
North Charleston, South Carolina

1

Mama knocked twice on my bedroom door. "There's a god-awful stench coming from in there," she said. "You need to take your bucket outside and empty it."

At one time, when I first started using the bucket as a toilet, the acrid air in my room had burned the inside of my nose and everything I ate and drank tasted like the smell of pee. But now, after months of constant exposure, I hardly noticed it at all. I was only aware, whenever I left my room, that the air outside it was different, thinner, crisper—different.

I heard the two-by-four Mama kept wedged under my doorknob fall hard, as usual, as if she had kicked it away, but its impact to the floor was muffled by the carpet. Like an angry fist blocked by a pillow. The sound of the two-by-four falling was always the same. Every morning, as I waited for her to come and let me out to go to school, or do my chores, I listened for it with both anticipation and dread, hoping one day it would be different. I kept thinking if the sound was different then maybe other things beyond the door might be different too.

As I made my way down the stairs, balancing the half-full bucket against my thigh, I noticed the house was quiet for a

Saturday. When I came to the bottom of the stairway, I looked around, and realized no one was home but Mama and me. I always got nervous when I was alone with her.

Passing the kitchen, I saw her leaning up against the counter stirring creamer into a cup of coffee. She hadn't been up long; she still had on a sleeping gown and her hair was matted to the back of her head. When I walked by her, she glanced up at me and tapped her spoon on the side of her cup. "Make sure you take it far away from the house," she said.

"Yes, ma'am," I yelled, on my way out the door.

Out in the backyard, I found a grassy area under a tree and sat the bucket down. I had learned if I dumped the pee all at once it spread quickly on the surface of the baked earth, and sometimes my feet got wet. Pouring slowly, I watched the bucket's contents seep into the grass and wrap its rusty fingers around the tree roots.

When I came back inside, Mama met me at the door. "I need some potatoes peeled for lunch," she said, and then went into the kitchen again.

After I returned the bucket to my room, I stood before her awaiting my next instructions. She pointed to a corner where she'd spread some newspaper on the floor. "Sit down over there," she said. Then she pulled a sack of potatoes from the pantry and plopped them beside me, along with a deep soup pan. She handed me a paring knife. "Now get to peeling."

Taking a potato from the sack, I started to work right away. Mama went over to the counter, picked up her coffee and walked back and forth in front of me. Sipping her coffee, she continued to pace the floor, staring at me, her steps getting faster and faster, as she became fueled by the caffeine.

I ignored her. Concentrated on the potato in my hand, on keeping the peeling the way she required it to be—thin enough to see through when she held it up to the light.

Finally, she stopped, tilted her head to one side. "I swear you get homelier every day," she said.

If I had been younger I would have cried, crushed by her words. But in the last couple of years I'd become much tougher. *So what,* I thought, acting as if I hadn't heard her. *I don't care what you think of me anymore.*

"I thought you might get prettier when you became a teenager, but I do believe you're even uglier than before." She paused, took a long drink of her coffee, allowing enough time for what she'd said to really sink in. "Honestly, I feel sorry for you because I don't know how you're going to make it on your own. I mean, *I* always had men standing in line to take care of me, but with your face I doubt you'll be able to find anyone."

Sliding the knife blade under the peel of a fresh potato, I tried to imagine her at thirteen, a bubbly cheerleader with a head full of shiny red curls and perfect skin. It was a stretch. She had gained about thirty pounds in the last year or so, and her hair was brassy and brittle from constant bleaching. The scar from her accident, deep and severe, slashed across her cheek like a lightning bolt.

For several minutes, she went on walking and talking and I continued to ignore her. Every so often, I caught a glimpse of her as she passed, but I didn't hear a word she was saying. The only sound I allowed into my head was the knife scraping across the potatoes.

When I had finished and there was a mountain of paper-thin peelings in front of me, Mama snatched up the pan filled with creamy, spotless potatoes. "Now pick up the papers and put them in the trash," she said. "I have another chore for you to do."

She pulled a brown paper grocery bag from a cabinet drawer and motioned for me to follow her into the family room. With her finger, she drew a series of small circles in the air above an area of the floor littered with crumpled potato chips. "I want you to pick up all the crumbs on the carpet in here. And don't stop until this whole room is clean."

She handed me the paper bag and I nodded my head, as if I understood her. But I didn't. I had never understood why she made me use my fingers to pick up specks of dirt and food crumbs from the floor when she had a perfectly good vacuum cleaner.

On her way back to the kitchen, she stopped in the hallway. "On second thought, start there," she said, pointing in the direction of the back door where there were dirt clods and mud ground into the carpet. "And then work your way up the hall into the family room."

I trudged down the hall, dragging the paper bag beside me. When I came to the top of the steps leading to the door, I sat and stared at the dirty carpet wondering where Daddy and the boys had gone. Wishing I were with them.

About ten minutes later, Mama came back to check on my progress and found me sitting down on the job. "What in hell do you think you're doing?" she asked, her voice reflecting disbelief more than anger.

Had it been a year, a month, or even a few days earlier, I would have been terrified of what she might do to me for disobeying her. I would have dropped to my knees and started picking up crumbs, scratching mud. But on this day, something was different. This day I didn't budge when I heard her coming.

"Answer me!" she shouted.

I didn't turn around.

Suddenly I heard the rapid pounding of her feet against the floor behind me. "Answer me!" she shouted again, but this time with her words came the blunt force of her foot in the small of my back. I felt a hot pain in my kidney. "I said answer me damn it!"

Out of the corner of my eye, I saw her cock her leg back to kick me again. But before she could deliver the blow, I sprang to my feet, grabbed her by one of her wrists and dug my fingers into the soft flesh of the underside of her forearm.

Looking down into her eyes, I tried to decipher what she was feeling from a facial expression I'd never before seen. I had known my mama at her darkest time, in her deepest pain. And, certainly, I'd witnessed her anger again and again. But never, under the safety of Daddy's six foot seven inch wingspan, had I known her to be afraid.

"My name is Tuesday, Mama!" I said, twisting her arm, slightly. "Say my name! Say it! Say Tuesday!"

The words had come out of my mouth, and yet, the voice I heard, full of vengeance and bitterness, sounded strangely foreign to my ears. One part of me was entirely detached from what was happening, as if I were watching some mean, crazed intruder hurting my mama. At the same time, another part was well aware of what I was doing, of every detail of the instant: the blood rushing through my head, the smell of coffee on her breath, her pulse throbbing under my hand.

"I'll *call you* what I damn well please!" A grimace cut across her face. "Take your hands off me!"

I tightened my grip. "Don't you think you've punished me enough, Mama? Don't you think I've suffered enough for what I did? I can't take it anymore! I *won't* take it anymore!"

She tugged her arm back, trying to pull free of my clutch. "Take your hands off me—now!" she demanded.

Then, in an instant, something—maybe it was the tone of her voice—caused the courage I had seconds earlier to desert me and I dropped her arm like it was a hot wire. And once again I became a frightened child, ready to obey her every command in the same instinctive way I had always obeyed her.

After what I'd just done, I expected her to attack me. This time I wanted her to. This time I'd asked for it, deserved it. I braced myself for the punch I knew was inevitable.

But nothing happened.

Maybe she had seen something in my eyes when I was squeezing her arm and knew if she made an attempt to hurt me again it would unleash all the rage I had pent up inside, the rage she had created. Maybe now she was scared of *me*.

She looked down at her arm and examined the purple crescents my fingernails had imprinted there. When she finally looked up again, I saw that her complexion was colorless, her bottom lip quivering. We stood face to face, stunned, as if neither of us was able to process what had happened, as if neither of us knew what to do next.

"Get out of my sight," she said, trying to sound in control with a voice that was thin and shaky. "Go to your room—now!"

Pushing past her, I bounded up the stairs, clearing two at a time. When I got in my room, I shut the door behind me and pressed my back up against it.

After a few minutes, I heard Mama wedge the two-by-four under my doorknob again. All at once, my legs gave out and I slid down to the floor. "I'm sorry, Mama!" I cried out to her, as she walked down the stairs. "I didn't mean it!"

OUR PERFECT FAMILY

2

I was sitting cross-legged on the floor in front of Audrey, holding one of her cold, stiff feet in my hands. Mama was beside me with the other foot, showing me how to use gentle pressure with my thumbs to roll away the loose, cheesy flesh from between Audrey's toes, and scratch off the more stubborn patches with my fingernails.

The dead skin that accumulated on Audrey's feet had to be tended to on a regular basis. Not because it itched, or was uncomfortable; she couldn't feel anything south of her hips anyway. And not because of how gross it looked, all yellow and crusty, but because of the smell—nauseatingly sweet, like meat when it first begins to go bad. If the skin wasn't cleared away, at least weekly, the smell of it would first permeate every surface in the bedroom Audrey and I shared, and then waft down the hallway, gradually claiming the rest of the house.

"It stinks," I whined.

"Then breathe through your mouth," Mama said.

"I *am* breathing through my mouth, and I can still smell it."

"Shush before you hurt your sister's feelings."

Mama always called Audrey my sister, but she wasn't really. She was only my half sister because she had a different father than my brothers and me. Mama said Audrey's father had deserted her after she got pregnant and she had to drop out of high school when she was only seventeen and take care of a baby all by herself.

She handed me a bottle of Rose Milk. "Try adding some of this."

I pumped a mound of the pink lotion into my palm, slathered it on my hands and began rolling away the skin on Audrey's feet, like Mama had showed me.

"Still stinks," I mumbled under my breath.

"*Tuesday,* not another word!"

I loved how Mama said my name in her syrupy, Southern way, like, *Tooos*-de. I loved my name too. According to Mama, I was named after a beautiful actress from the sixties, Tuesday Weld.

"I had my mind all set to name you Marilyn, you know, after Marilyn Monroe," Mama had explained. "Then a few hours before you were born, out of the clear blue, one of the nurses at the hospital up and asked me, 'Has anybody ever told you that you resemble Tuesday Weld?' Well, I figured it had to be a sign. I mean, it was the perfect name for you, because you were born that night, and it was on a Tuesday!" She leaned in to me and whispered, "Actually, it was seven minutes past twelve, Wednesday morning, but it was dark out, so it still felt like Tuesday to me."

Mama liked to name her kids after famous people. Audrey was named after Audrey Hepburn, and she wanted to name my older brother, Nick, after Charlton Heston. But Daddy stepped in and vetoed the idea, insisting his firstborn be his namesake.

He couldn't think of anything to save my younger brother, James Dean, though.

Mama got up, lit a cherry incense stick and stuck it in an empty bud vase on Audrey's dresser. As I watched the thin strands of smoke spiral up into the room, I thought about death.

My only experience with death had been the previous summer. It was hot that day, hot enough, as we say in the South, to fry bacon on the sidewalk. My brothers, Nick Jr., Jimmy D. and I had brought our game of hide-and-seek inside our house to cool off under the air-conditioner.

It was my turn to hide. I was standing in the living room trying to decide between behind the couch or under the drop leaf table, when I got the idea in my head that it would be neat if I could slip outside and hide in the bushes in front of the house. I was sure my brothers would never look for me there.

I could hear them in the kitchen counting...eighty-nine... ninety...ninety-one. I ran over to the door and eased it open. As I stepped onto the front porch, Jacque, Mama's toy poodle, came from nowhere, weaved through my legs and dashed out into the yard.

Jacque, a hyper dog, had always been confined to a leash whenever we took him out because Mama was afraid he might run into the road. Now, unrestrained in the open yard for the first time, he was crazy with his freedom, darting in all directions.

I knew Mama would be upset with me if she found out I had let Jacque loose, so I chased after him, thinking I could catch him and bring him back inside before she realized what had happened. But he was too fast, and I was no match for his sharp side-to-side movement. I was determined, though, and driven by my fear of getting into trouble. After a feverish pursuit, resulting in two grass-skinned knees, I did manage to trap him between some bushes and the mailbox. Quickly I dove to grab him, but he dodged away from me. I dove again, and this time he ran through the bushes and into the road, right in the path of a yellow Volkswagen Beetle.

The next thing I remember is hearing three sounds at once: the screech of car brakes, a yelp, and a thud. I rushed into the road, the asphalt scorching the bottoms of my bare feet, and found Jacque lying in front of the Volkswagen, motionless. He looked like he had stretched out for an afternoon nap, except his tongue hung from the side of his open mouth and blood trickled from one nostril.

Daddy, Mama and my brothers came running out of the house to see what all the commotion was about. Mama let out a painful gasp when she saw what had happened, and then covered her mouth with both hands. Daddy bent down and felt of Jacque's neck, pronounced him dead and scooped up his limp body from the road.

We all, including the teenage girl who was driving the Volkswagen, followed Daddy into the backyard and formed a quiet circle around him while he dug a grave under a mimosa tree. We stood there, in awkward silence, for what seemed like the longest time, watching him toss shovel after shovel of dirt over Jacque's body.

Finally, I couldn't take it anymore. "Daddy, did Jacque hurt when he got hit by the car?"

Everybody turned and looked at me at once.

Daddy stopped digging, wiped the sweat from his brow with the back of his wrist, and propped one arm on the shovel. "Oh no, honey, it all happened so fast he didn't feel a thing."

"How did he get outside in the first place?" Mama asked no one in particular.

"He ran through my legs when I was going out the door!" I piped up. "He was so fast I didn't even see him coming!"

"What were you doing going out the front door?" she asked.

"We were playing hide-and-seek and I wanted to hide in the bushes."

"You know better, Tuesday!" she scolded. "You know you're not allowed to play in the front yard!"

"I'm sorry, Mama!"

"Sorry isn't good enough this time, young lady. Maybe if you had done as you were told, Jacque wouldn't have been killed!"

She turned her back to me and walked into the house. It would have hurt less if she'd whacked me across the face with the shovel.

In the next few days, Jacque, who had once been ignored by everyone in the family except Mama, suddenly became the greatest dog that ever lived.

"I miss him so much!" Nick said. "Remember when we gave him a bath and he shook soap bubbles all over us?"

"He was so cute when he was wet!" Jimmy D. added.

Mama was truly heartsick, though. She never came right out and blamed me for Jacque's death, but she didn't have to. I could tell by the cold distance she created between us.

With time, Mama's sadness over Jacque' death began to wane, and she threw away his squeaky toys, and the blanket he had slept on in the garage. With every remnant of him gone from our sight, it didn't take long for our family to forget all about him and turn our attention and affection to our other dog, a cocker spaniel mix named Rusty.

The burnt part of the incense became too heavy to support itself any longer and fell, splattering gray ashes on top of the dresser. It was in that instant that it hit me, with absolute certainty, that I wanted what had happened to Jacque to happen to Audrey. I knew it wasn't likely she would be hit by a car, but I wanted her to die somehow and for someone to come and take her body away, along with all her stuff. After her death, Mama and Daddy would be sad for a while, like they were with Jacque, but they would get over the loss, and in time, forget all about her and turn their attention to me, their other daughter.

Everyone said it should have already happened anyway. They said it was a miracle Audrey had lived to be sixteen. She caught the polio virus when she was a baby, and according to Mama, ever since then she had been either sick or on the brink of sickness. And there had been countless trips to the emergency room. Once she stopped breathing in the ambulance on the way to the hospital and the paramedics had to perform a tracheotomy to keep her alive. The procedure left a bright pink heart-shaped scar smack in the middle of her throat, a fitting reminder that she had cheated death.

Audrey and her sickness consumed far too much of my mama's life, far too much of my life. Without her, our family could go anywhere we wanted, places we had never been able to go before, like the theater, without worrying about whether or not we could take Audrey's wheelchair. I thought if only she were gone, our lives would be perfect, our family would be perfect. But I was only seven years old; I didn't know how to make someone die.

3

"Good morning, angel!" Mama said, as she stood in the doorway yawning. She entered the room, tying the belt of her house robe.

Audrey's face lit up. "Morning, Mama!"

Mama passed by my bed on her way to Audrey's. "And look who else is awake!" I leaped up and ran to her side, flinging my arms around her waist.

With me glued to her hip, she went over to the window and raised the blinds. "How are you feeling this morning?" she asked Audrey.

A shaft of sunlight shot across Audrey's eyes. She snapped them shut. "Just fine."

Mama looked down at me and stroked the back of my head. "Tuesday, do you want to help me get ready for your sister's bath?"

I didn't. I hated helping with Audrey's bath. I hated anything to do with taking care of her. But I loved being around Mama. "Sure," I answered, faking enthusiasm and followed her into the bathroom.

Our bathroom had barely enough space for both of us to squeeze into at once. Every room in our house in Spring

Hill, Tennessee was small, and our family of six was cramped. A three-bedroom ranch was the best Daddy could afford on a teacher's salary, but when it came to the necessities in life, we never wanted for a thing. At night, we went to bed with our bellies full—Mama knew how to make a bag of pinto beans and a ten-pound sack of potatoes go a long way—and we kids always had at least two outfits and a new pair of shoes to start school every year.

Mama pulled two rusty-edged, white enamel washbowls from under the bathroom sink and filled them with warm water from the tap. One bowl of water would be used to wet the sponge and lather the soap for Audrey's bath, and the other, to rinse the soap off.

"Why can't you put Audrey in the bathtub?" I asked.

"Now, Tuesday, you know the answer to that question. You know your sister can't sit by herself."

"She can sit by herself in her wheelchair," I pointed out. "Why can't she sit in the tub? I'll help you put her in."

"I've explained this to you before, Tuesday. Audrey's muscles don't work, that's why I have to strap her in her chair to keep her from falling over."

"But she doesn't even try to sit up. Maybe if you didn't strap her in she would try to sit on her own."

"That's enough, young lady!" she snapped. "Now hush up talking like that before she hears you." She lifted one of the bowls of water and started for the bathroom door. "You get the soap and the towels and I'll come back for the other bowl."

I took the towels and soap to Mama and she arranged them, along with the wash bowls and a sponge, on Audrey's bedside table. Then she undressed Audrey and draped one of the towels over her lower body for privacy. She dipped the sponge into one of the bowls of water and rubbed it against the bar of soap.

"You're a living angel; that's what you are," Mama said soothingly, as she eased the sponge onto Audrey's chest and worked it in a circular motion.

"Oh, Mama, you always say that," Audrey said.

"That's because it's true, honey!"

Mama lifted Audrey's right arm—which was nothing more than a misshapen mass of flabby flesh dangling at her side—and ran the sponge under it a few times. When she was satisfied, she moved on to the left arm. We called Audrey's left arm her good arm, because it was leaner than the right and stronger in comparison. But it wasn't of much use to her because her left hand was rigid and clamped shut. Still, she tried to do simple tasks with her good arm, to comb her hair and brush her teeth, but it was a major struggle and she was always exhausted afterward. Whenever she attempted to eat on her own, most of her food ended up on the floor, and when she went to pick up a drink, she knocked it over instead.

Audrey was shivering, and her lips were turning purple. "I'm getting cold," she said.

Mama quickened her pace, sliding the sponge down the sides of Audrey's thick torso. "You feel okay, don't you?" she asked, reaching up and touching the back of her hand to Audrey's forehead. "I mean, you don't feel sick, do you?"

"No, Mama, I'm not sick, I'm just cold."

"You need to start doing your frog breathing exercise again."

"But I feel fine."

"You know as well as I do that could change at any minute. Besides, there's a flu going around right now and you know you catch *everything*."

"But I hate frog breathing; it's hard!"

I'd seen Audrey do her breathing exercise before. All she had to do was suck air into her lungs in tiny gulps, hold it for a while and then let it out again. Gulp, gulp, gulp, and exhale. I thought she wasn't trying, like I thought she wasn't trying to sit on her own.

"Frog breathing isn't hard, Audrey," I butted in. "You're just lazy!"

"You shut up!" Audrey fired back. "You don't know nothing anyway. You're just a little twirp!"

Mama gave me a stern look as she removed the towel that was draped over Audrey's legs. From the waist up, Audrey was a fully developed sixteen-year-old girl, but her legs never caught up with the rest of her body. They were frail and shapeless with prominent, zipper-like scars that started at her knees and went all the way to her ankles. The scars were from an operation she had where surgeons removed bones from her legs and put them in her back to correct her severe scoliosis. The surgery left another deeper, fleshier scar that ran the length of her back.

"Audrey, honey, I know frog breathing is hard," Mama said. "Tuesday doesn't know what it's like to have weak lungs. But even though it's hard, you still have to do it."

When Mama finished Audrey's bath, she dressed her in a blue sweatshirt, black polyester pants and bobby socks, which she folded down at the top, making sure they were perfectly even, as if it mattered. I couldn't figure out why she took so much care in dressing Audrey when nobody outside the family ever saw her anyway, except the doctor when it was time for her check-up, and a tutor who came two or three days a week.

Mama stepped back and took a look. "Now, you're all set. Ready to get into your chair?"

Audrey nodded, and Mama slid one arm under her neck and the other behind her knees. "Here we go," she said. "On three." They counted together, as Mama lifted Audrey from her bed and carefully lowered her into her wheelchair. "You can watch television now," Mama said, bending to flip the footplates of the wheelchair down. "But later on, you're doing your breathing exercises." She gathered up the towels and washbowls, and I followed close behind her as she started to leave the room. She stopped when we got to the door. "Tuesday, you stay in here and keep your sister company. I've got a mountain of laundry to do and I don't need a tagalong."

I stomped back over to Audrey, sat on the floor in front of the television set and pouted.

Later, like we did every Saturday afternoon, Audrey and I watched her favorite show, *American Bandstand*. As the teenagers on television did the funky chicken, and the swim, Audrey rocked her head back and forth and waved her good arm around, trying to mimic the dancers as best she could.

When it was over, she wanted to see what was going on out in the backyard, so I pushed her to the window. I propped myself on the side of her wheelchair, and we stared outside together without saying a word.

It was an unseasonably warm day for the middle of February. Mama was taking advantage of the early sampling of spring to hang the clean laundry out on the clothesline. Jimmy D. was riding his bicycle in a tight circle on the back patio, the training wheels squeaking as he went around and around. His golden blonde hair, which Mama had recently given a Beatle cut, was glistening in the sunlight. He and I both had the same color hair that Daddy had when he was a boy. We both had green eyes too, like Daddy's. My older brother, Nick, was farther out in the yard playing croquet with a couple of the neighborhood boys. He favored Mama, with amber eyes and strawberry-blonde hair.

Audrey soon got bored with watching people do things she couldn't and decided she wanted to listen to one of her Beatles albums. The one way she was like every other teenage girl in 1970 was that she worshipped the Beatles.

I had no more than wheeled her over to the record player when she said, "Play 'Get Back' first."

"Wait a minute," I said, trying to slip the album from its cover. "Let me get it out."

She giggled. "It's my favorite song."

As if I didn't know. She had me play it most every day, over and over. I had the lyrics memorized and knew exactly where it was on the album too. "I know it's your favorite!" I said, and put the needle in the right groove on the first try.

"Tuesday, can you dance?"

"I don't know; I guess so."

"Well, let's see you try. Start moving around like they do on *American Bandstand*."

I tried to remember the dancers I'd seen on television. I twisted my butt, and shook my head back and forth. My long, stringy hair stung my cheeks as it slapped across them. "Like this?"

A big smile spread across Audrey's face. "Yeah, that's right!" she squealed. "Keep it up!"

Seeing her happy filled my heart with eagerness, eagerness to please her, to keep her smiling. I shook my hips with even more verve, this time trying with great concentration to hit the rhythm of the song. But her smile, rare as a lunar eclipse, was big and bright one minute, and then, all at once gone, sinking behind the darkness that always claimed her.

"Move your arms," she said.

I lifted my arms, but I wasn't sure what she wanted me to do with them, and she couldn't show me, so I did the first thing that came to mind: I flapped them, like a bird flaps its wings. "This way?" I asked.

"No, silly, not like a chicken! Swing them from side to side, you know, like the dancers on *Bandstand*!"

I swung my arms to and fro in front of my body.

"Yeah, that's it! Now twist your hips!" She directed her eyes down to my waist, then back up to my face again. "And bend your knees some too."

She watched me for a minute, and then leaned back in her chair. She closed her eyes and began swaying her head to the music, as if in her mind she was dancing along with me.

I became lost in a fantasy of my own. I closed my eyes and imagined I was a ballerina, like the tiny one in the jewelry box on Audrey's dresser. As I arched my back and lifted my arms, forming a perfect circle above my head, in my mind's eye, I could see my graceful reflection in a diamond-shaped mirror surrounded by blue satin. I twirled all around the room, twirled and twirled, until I bumped into my bed and fell backwards onto the floor, landing smack on my bottom, legs splayed.

Audrey opened her eyes and laughed when she saw me. Embarrassed, I jumped up. But the minute I stood on my feet, the room started to spin around me and I fell back down again. She laughed even harder, which caused me to start laughing too. The more I laughed, the more she laughed. Our laughter was robust and fearless. It sprang from a place somewhere deep inside of us, a place we didn't even know existed, and gave us a glimpse of what things might have been like between us had we not been so isolated by our differences.

All at once she stopped laughing and fell forward in her chair. She was top-heavy, so she lost her balance often, but still, each time it happened she freaked out. "Help me!" she called out to me, her face red from straining to hold herself up.

Still dizzy, I struggled to my feet, but instead of running to help her, like I usually did, I stood there watching her from across the room. A vision of her tumbling into the floor face first popped in my head. "Try to pull yourself back on your own," I said.

"I can't, stupid!" she shouted. "Help me up! Hurry, I'm falling out of my chair!"

"Yes, you can!" I insisted. "Try really hard!"

"Mama!" she cried. "Maaa-maaa!"

Through the window, I could see Mama in the backyard hanging sheets on the line. She plucked a clothespin from her mouth and pinned the corner of a pillowcase, and then picked up the empty laundry basket and started for the house.

A searing bolt of fear shot through me. "Okay, I'm coming." I rushed to Audrey's side and pushed her up straight in her chair.

"Now fix me so I won't fall over again," she said.

Having done it many times before, I knew exactly what she meant. She wanted me to reposition her in her seat so her weight would be more evenly distributed. First I secured the latch that locked the wheels of the chair, and then got behind her, wrapped my arms firmly around her chest and gave her a sharp tug up and back, using my weight for leverage.

Then I walked around her chair and stood in front of her. I clamped my hands together in a begging position. "Don't tell Mama, Audrey. Please, please don't tell her. She would be mad at me for letting you fall."

Before she could answer, Mama walked in and lifted the arm of the record player, stopping the Beatles in mid-lyric. "Okay, angel, it's time for your breathing exercises."

4

Mama had an irrational fear of germs. She kept brown bottles of Lysol handy in each room of the house so she could wipe everything down daily. Now, frantic with worry Audrey might catch the flu that was going around, she had become even more of a fanatic. In addition to saturating every surface in the house with the Lysol, she insisted we all scrub our hands with grainy Lava soap several times a day until our skin was raw. But still, all her precautions weren't enough to keep the Hong Kong flu from invading our home. Jimmy D. was the first to get it, and within a week he had passed it on to Nick.

To keep their germs from spreading to Audrey, Mama quarantined the boys and issued them old dish cloths to use as makeshift masks, instructing them to tie them around their faces, gangster-style, and wear them whenever they came out of their room.

Because I shared a bedroom with Audrey, I had always been expected to keep an eye on her to make sure her breathing didn't become erratic. Now that the flu was a real threat, Mama asked even more from me. "I'm going to need your help with your sister now more than ever before," she said. "If she starts breathing strange, or coughing, or doing anything out of the ordinary, you need to come and let me know immediately." She reached down and cupped my chin in her hand in a stern but loving way, directing my eyes at hers. "This is very important, Tuesday. I'm counting on you."

She and I alternated sitting with Audrey to watch for any signs that she might be getting the flu. My turn began when I got in from school and lasted until ten o'clock, and then Mama came in and took over for the rest of the night.

During my shift, I had trouble staying awake because I had to get up early every morning to go to school. I complained to Mama, telling her I was too tired to watch Audrey anymore and that I was getting in trouble for falling asleep in class.

"I know you're tired, sweetie," she said. "I'm tired too, but if Audrey gets this flu she could die. You don't want your sister to die, do you?"

One night, as I lay in bed watching Audrey, I noticed that I felt even more tired than usual, so tired my muscles ached. I wanted nothing more than to sleep, but I knew Mama would get mad at me if Audrey got sick and I didn't tell her. I had to think of something to make me stay awake until my watch was up. Then I remembered a piece of bubble-gum someone at school had given me. I grabbed my backpack from the floor at the foot of my bed, dug around in it until I found the gum, and then popped it into my mouth.

The sugar gave me an instant burst of energy. I sat up and took my favorite pink troll doll down from the shelf above my bed and stroked its hair, searching the room around me for something to entertain my eye and keep me from falling asleep.

Our bedroom was the largest of the three in the house, but it seemed small because it was too crowded with oversized furniture: Audrey's full canopy bed, an executive-style writing desk, a console television and a triple dresser. Crammed in a cubbyhole, were my twin bed and the chest of drawers that housed my clothes. My toys—Barbie dolls, Little Kiddles, and troll collection—were all displayed on two shelves above my bed.

The rest of the space in the room was filled with Audrey's stuff. She had gotten everything she'd ever asked for, most of which she didn't need, or couldn't use. Like the electric organ she wasn't even able to play. It was covered with dusty board games that had never been opened. Posters of the Beatles papered the walls, and all around the floor were tall stacks of their albums and teen magazines that threatened to topple over whenever someone brushed by them.

She had a ridiculously large collection of stuffed animals: a parrot perched in a swing on top of the television set; a monkey with a banana in its hand dangled from one of the posts of her bed, and stuffed in every inch of remaining space were a dozen or more teddy bears. Some nights I became frightened, as I lay awake surrounded by these creatures that often appeared wicked and threatening in the shadows of the half-dark.

My bed was situated directly across from Audrey's. From there, I watched her sleep. A small lamp on her nightstand, draped with a sheer, pink scarf, served as her night light and so Mama could find her way in the dark when she came in to check on her. The soft light from the lamp washed over Audrey's face, giving her skin a rosy glow and a deceptive illusion of health.

A little before nine o'clock, she woke up and looked over at me in my bed. "What are you chewing on?" she asked.

"Just some bubble gum; some kid at school gave it to me."

"Got anymore?"

"Nope, only this one piece," I said, blowing a big bubble to tease her.

"Can I have part of yours?"

"It's all chewed up, and most of the flavor is gone."

"I don't care. My mouth is dry. Bite me off a piece."

"If you're thirsty I can hold your water while you sip it."

"I don't want water; I want something sweet. *Please,* Tuesday."

I bit my gum into two pieces and put one between her lips.

She chewed it for a minute. "The flavor is all gone now," she said. "Get a tissue so I can spit it out."

Daddy came in, as he did every night before he went to sleep, and gave Audrey a kiss. Then he walked over to my bed and kissed me. "Night, sweetheart," he said. "Your mama will be in soon so you can get some rest."

Audrey fell back to sleep, and soon her breathing became even. Weary from fatigue, for another hour, I watched her chest rise and descend, rise and descend and dreamt about what my life might be like if her lungs deflated and collapsed, and her chest never came back up again. *I could go outside and play with Nick and Jimmy D., like a normal kid. I could finally be a normal kid.*

I was sure Audrey would be better off dead too. I thought of the pathetic way she flopped her arms around, and her scrawny legs that may as well have been two tree limbs propped in front of her for all the good they were. I remembered her "down days," as Mama called them, when she sat staring out the window for hours, tears streaming from her eyes. Whenever I asked her what was wrong, she never said, but I knew she must have been crying because she was trapped in a body that couldn't do what she wanted it to, crying for all she would never experience. She was in pain from her sadness, in pain from her illness. She had to be tired of pain.

5

The following morning, I woke up with a scratchy throat and a headache, and my arms and legs were weak and sore. I told Mama, and right away, she moved me and my bed into my brothers' room.

Daddy got sick the same day, and Mama no longer allowed him to go anywhere near Audrey. Like she had done with my brothers, she gave both him and me masks to wear whenever we had to get out of our beds to go to the bathroom.

Two days later, despite the quarantine, the masks, the endless scrubbing of our skin with Lava soap, and all the bottles of Lysol we went through, Audrey started coughing and running a slight fever.

Daddy called the family doctor, who made a special trip out to the house to examine her. After a thorough check, he confirmed that she did in fact have the Hong Kong flu. Luckily, she was only in the early stages and the doctor didn't think it was necessary for her to go into the hospital. He felt confident that with the proper medication and provided we kept a close watch over her, she would be more comfortable at home, at least for the time being.

Mama put a vaporizer beside Audrey's bed and lined up bottles of medicine on her nightstand. Since the damage had already been done, I was moved back to our room so I could help with watching her again.

After a few days of taking the medications the doctor had prescribed, Audrey's condition improved and she began sleeping through the night. We thought she was getting better, until one night, I heard her making a peculiar sound in her sleep. She purred when she drew air into her lungs and then wheezed as she released it again. Right away, I reported this new development to Mama, who rushed to Audrey's side.

Daddy came in to feel Audrey's brow, checking for a rise in her temperature. He couldn't hide the worry on his face.

"I don't know how she could have gotten the flu, Nick," Mama said. "I was so careful."

"Rose, there's no sense in worrying about that now."

"I know it's not helping matters."

"You of all people should know how tough Audrey is. Think of all she's been through. She's not going to let this flu get her down. She's a fighter, always has been, always will be."

"But she's been so tired lately." Mama's voice cracked from fatigue and from being on the verge of crying. "What if she's too tired, Nick? What if she's tired of fighting? I don't know what I would do if I lost her."

Daddy put his arm around Mama's shoulders and held her close. "You're not going to lose her, Rosie."

Mama turned to me and said in a slight voice, "Go to sleep now, Tuesday. You must be exhausted." Then she crawled in bed with Audrey, and Daddy pulled the covers up around both of them.

I closed my eyes, but as tired as I was, I couldn't sleep. Something dreadful had found its way into my head and was gnawing at my brain—the thought that I might have been the one who gave Audrey the flu. That maybe the reason I had felt achy that night when I was watching her was because I was already sick before Mama moved me into the boys' room.

Then I remembered the bubble-gum I'd shared with Audrey and my eyes popped wide open. *The bubble-gum! It had to be the bubble-gum!* I knew if Mama, with her phobia of germs, ever found out I'd given Audrey my already chewed bubble-gum she would kill me. I could never tell her, and I wouldn't have to because Audrey would soon be well again and no harm would have been done.

6

The next day, Audrey slept most of the time. That night, her breathing was heavy and husky, and a deep, rattling cough often interrupted her sleep. She had a cup on the nightstand beside her bed to spit out the profuse amounts of phlegm her lungs were producing. The mucus, which at the beginning of her sickness had been pale yellow and then gradually turned green, now had a rusty tint to it.

Four days after Audrey got the flu, she woke up with a high fever. Mama wrapped her in towels drenched in ice water, but her temperature wouldn't drop a degree. That's when Daddy declared it was time to take her to the emergency room. He went next door and asked a neighbor to come over and sit with my brothers and me, while Mama got a few of Audrey's things together.

Audrey was admitted to the hospital that day, a Tuesday, and by the following Saturday, on March 3, 1970, she had died.

During the funeral, and long after the service was over, Mama clung to Audrey's casket and sobbed. It took hours for Daddy to pry her away, and when he finally did, she refused to leave. When it began to get dark out, he had to pick her up and force into the car to take her home.

All through the night, she moaned in agony and screamed out Audrey's name. By the next morning, she had cried so much her face was swollen to twice its normal size and her eyes were nothing but narrow slits surrounded by puffy tissue. Daddy had to call the doctor to come out to the house and give her a sedative shot to calm her down just so she could sleep.

Relatives, most of them I had never met before, came to show their sympathy to my parents for the loss of their child. Some of them said things like, "Poor Rose has been through so much." Others talked about Audrey, and how she'd never had a life at all. "She's in a better place now," one of them said. "Now her pain is over."

The neighbors brought casseroles and cakes and plates of sandwiches, so many we ran out of surfaces to sit them on. When the counters in the kitchen were full, we had to start putting dishes of food in the living room on Mama's treasured Duncan Fife coffee table. Normally, she would have thrown a fit, but she was so out of it, she didn't even care.

In the days to follow, she lost her appetite completely. She wouldn't talk to anyone. She even stopped bathing. Heavily sedated, she spent most of her time sitting on Audrey's bed, gazing out into the open space, as if she were looking at something none of the rest of us could see.

Daddy took Audrey's death rough too. He had been her father since she was an infant and he loved her as if she were his own blood. I never saw him cry, although I suspected he did when no one was watching. He moved about the house like a massive zombie, his eyelids rimmed in red and circled in gray from lack of sleep. He busied himself with handling all the funeral arrangements, looking after the family, the cooking and cleaning, trying to keep some semblance of order amidst all the madness.

As for me, I struggled with my own secret hell from the guilt of having given my sister the flu that killed her. I had thought her death would be best for everyone, but now, seeing how sad it made Mama and Daddy, I realized I'd been wrong. And I could not move past the absoluteness of it all, of Audrey being gone for good. I would never see her again, or hear her laugh like she had when I danced for her. I kept thinking about that day and how much fun we had.

I asked Daddy if Audrey had suffered when she died and he promised me she hadn't. "She suffered enough in her lifetime, so I'm sure God, in His mercy, took her without pain."

Knowing this made me feel better.

Days crept by after the funeral, with Mama showing no indication of improvement. She seemed like she was no longer concerned with caring for herself or the family. She continued to require sedative medication for her nerves, which made her sleep most of the time. When she wasn't sleeping, she was groggy, wandering through the house, aimlessly, with glassy eyes and a vacant stare.

She formed an odd attachment to a stuffed angel she had taken off one of the floral arrangements at the funeral. She cuddled it in her arms like a baby and sometimes sang it lullabies. "You're my angel and I love you," she whispered to the doll as if it were Audrey. "You're an angel, and you don't even know it, my angel unaware."

Mama had Daddy move my bed back in with my brothers so she could spend her days in Audrey's room alone. None of us were allowed to go in there because Mama was afraid we would move something and she wanted everything to remain exactly as Audrey had left it. My brothers and I hovered outside the closed bedroom door, lost. Without Mama, our lives had no rhythm, no direction.

After weeks of gently coaxing, Daddy was able to convince her to comb her hair and put on lipstick. He somehow managed to wean her from the angel doll too. After a few weeks more, she began expressing an interest in my brothers and me again and to resemble her former self.

With Mama close to being back to normal, it was time for us to get on with our lives as a family. To afford us more space in the house, Daddy finished out the basement so we could use it as a den. Nothing fancy, just some indoor/outdoor carpet on the concrete floor and a coat of white paint on the cinder block walls. He bought a small television set to put down in the den, as well as a couple of beanbag chairs. An old mattress was propped up against the wall, in case anyone wanted to lie on the floor, and it was the perfect place for Daddy's well-worn recliner that Mama had banished to the basement years earlier.

We called our new room a den, but it was more of a playroom for us kids and a retreat for Daddy. Mama didn't like the den. She claimed the floor was too cold and hard to her feet and she had no comfortable furniture to sit in down there.

Mama did her part to make more living space for the family too. She agreed to clear out Audrey's old bedroom so the boys could move in, and that meant I could take over their room and have it all to myself. At last, everything was working out as I had envisioned it would.

7

By the time my eighth birthday came around on July, 11, Mama was feeling much better. That morning, she woke me early and told me she had a special day planned for me. I followed her to her room and sat on the edge of her bed, waiting for her to get dressed.

She let her housecoat slide from her shoulders and tossed it onto a chair. Wearing nothing but her bra and panties, she dug through her drawers until she found her favorite red shell. She pulled it on over her head, tossed her curls back into shape and then squeezed into a pair of dark denim Bermuda shorts. She walked over to her vanity and sat on the padded bench in front of it. I jumped down from the bed and sat beside her, like I always did when she put on her makeup.

She picked up her brush with the mother-of-pearl handle, pulled it through her hair a couple of times and arranged a few wayward curls around her face. She slid open her red box of cake mascara and using the tiny black brush inside, applied some to her lashes. Then she selected, from the drawer of her vanity, the perfect shade of lipstick to match her shell and traced it along the lines of her full lips as she pursed them in an *O* shape. After a quick quality check in the mirror, she plucked a tissue from the dispenser and kissed it, leaving a bright red imprint of her mouth.

"There," she said springing to her feet. "Now let's tend to the Birthday Girl." She went over to her closet and pulled out a box wrapped in purple paper and tied with a yellow ribbon. My heart pounded with excitement when I realized it was a present for me. "I'm going to let you open this now. It's something special I picked out for you."

I took the present from her, tore through the paper, ripped apart the box and pulled out what was inside. It was a sun-suit that tied at the shoulders, red with black polka dots.

"I love it, Mama!" I stripped out of my pajamas right there so I could put it on and wear it for the rest of the day. "Thank you!"

"You're welcome, sweetheart."

For lunch, Mama made corndogs and macaroni and cheese, my two favorite foods, and for dessert, she baked a German chocolate cake, also my favorite. She adorned the cake with eight pink candles, lit them and then turned out the lights. Everyone in the family sang "Happy Birthday," as she brought my cake over to the kitchen table.

After we ate, I opened my other gift—a new troll doll with hair striped the colors of the rainbow—to add to my already large collection. Then Daddy, Nick, Jimmy D. and I all went outside. Daddy was finally going to make good on his promise to build us a tree house in a sprawling mimosa out in the backyard. Mama stayed behind and picked up the kitchen. It had been over four months since Audrey's death and she still hadn't left the house.

Out in the yard, I found a patch of soft grass and sat to make a dandelion necklace. Before too long, I heard the familiar sound of the back screen door, creak open, and then snap shut. In the far corner of the yard, Daddy and the boys stopped what they were doing and looked toward the house.

Out walked Mama, pressing the palm of her hand against the sun's glare. "My lands," she said. "At first I thought you were a big ol' ladybug out there in the grass! You look just like one in your new dotted sun-suit!"

I giggled at the thought. "Oh, Mama, you're silly!"

She picked up her lounger, which had been leaning against the outside of the house since last summer, unfolded it and situated it facing the sun. She lay down and stretched out with one leg hanging off the side and her bare foot resting on the concrete patio beneath her, as if at any minute she might get up and go back inside.

"Ladybug," she said as she rolled up her shorts so she could get some sun on her legs. "Hmm, now that's a good nickname for you. I think I'll call you that from now on." She tucked her shell up under her bra in front to expose her stomach, leaned her head back on the lounger and shut her eyes.

A grin crept onto my face. *Mama's back.*

I was about halfway done with my dandelion necklace when Daddy and the boys started making some loud noise hammering on the tree house. Mama raised her head and looked in their direction. Then she looked at me. "You sure have been out there in that grass for a long time, Ladybug. What are you doing, anyway?"

"Making a necklace," I said. "It's a present for somebody."

"Who could you be making a present for, it's *your* birthday."

"It's a surprise."

She smiled and the specks of copper in her eyes sparkled. She put her head back and rested it against the lounger again, her smooth face soaking in the sunlight.

Lana Page, the lady who lived next door, came out of her house and walked up to the chain-link fence between her yard and ours. "Hidy, Rose," she called out to Mama.

Mama lifted her head. "Hey, hon!"

Mama called everyone "honey" or "hon," and her favorite phrase was "bless your heart." Daddy said she was such a sweet talker she could call somebody a scum-sucking bitch, begin the sentence with "hon," tack "bless your heart" on the end, and they would think they were getting a compliment.

Mama had always been one to keep to herself. Even at her best, when she went out into the yard she was willing to talk only briefly with the ladies in the neighborhood about light subjects, such as fashion or cooking.

She hated nosey people and if someone overstepped her tight boundaries, she was quick to shift the conversation so they wouldn't have an opportunity to pry into her life. If that didn't work, she would suddenly act like she smelled beans burning, even if she wasn't cooking beans at all, and then take off running into the house to tend to them. Growing up, I never once saw my mama socialize with the neighbors without a fence in front of her and an imaginary pot of beans cooking on the stove.

"I'm fixin' to put on my bathing suit and lay in the sun," said Lana. "Why don't you come over and join me?"

"Oh, honey," said Mama, cupping her hand over her eyes to form a visor against the sun. "I'm not baring this pale body!"

Lana chuckled. "Don't be silly, Rose, you look great!"

Mama brushed off Lana's compliment. "Now, if I had your figure, Lana," she said, stringing out her sweet words like she was stringing taffy from her mouth, "Pale or not, I'd put on a bikini every day and strut all around this yard!"

"Oh, Rose, shut up! Come on, get your suit on and visit with me for a while. We'll catch up on some girl talk."

"I would Lana, really, but I've got to get up from here in a minute and make these hungry young'uns some supper. I've got pinto beans on the stove right now."

"Okay, then." Lana turned and walked back toward her house. "But the offer stands if you change your mind."

Most of our neighbors who lived on Maplewood Drive were like Lana, Southern small-town friendly, waving whenever they saw you, whether they knew you or not, stopping occasionally to chat. She and her husband, Jack, like all the young couples that lived on our street, were typical middle class of the seventies. The men were dominant heads of their households, responsible for the financial support of their families, and most of the wives were content to be homemakers and stay-at-home moms. Every couple had at least two children, many of which were around the same age. On summer afternoons, the smell of burgers grilling filled the air, the badminton nets went up, the croquet sets came out, and the yards were crawling with happy kids.

Our neighbors were friendly, but they were also aware of the boundaries that separated their private lives from one another—invisible boundaries, but still as impassable as the chain-link fences between their yards. They didn't press too hard to get into your business because they didn't want you poking around in theirs. That was the Southern way, the way Mama said it should be. She said it was of no concern to anyone what went on in the privacy of her home.

8

It started out as a typical summer day for us. Daddy went to work and Mama did her chores around the house. My brothers and I played out in the yard until about noon, when a steamy rain came from out of clear skies, forcing us back inside.

Mama brought out the Clue game to keep us occupied, and served up what was left of my birthday cake. When Daddy got home from work, we ate supper and then he and the boys went down to the new den, while I stayed upstairs with Mama in her bedroom.

She decided to take one of her long bubble baths. While she was soaking in the tub, I sat at her vanity and fingered the perfumes she had displayed on a gold filigree tray. The delicate jewel-toned bottles of many shapes and sizes intrigued my eye. I picked up each one and sprayed my neck twice, like I'd seen her do.

I went over to the closet, pulled out her black silk robe and put it on over my clothes and then slipped my feet into her furry pink house slippers that were on the floor directly beneath it. With the robe trailing behind me, I modeled in front of the mirror, striking various glamorous poses, trying to mimic the beautiful women I'd seen in the Sears catalogue.

When I got bored, I decided to join the rest of the family down in the den. When I came to the bottom of the stairs, I saw that Daddy and Jimmy D. had the mattress on the floor and they were playing the flying game. The flying game was something Daddy had invented to entertain Nick when he was a toddler. At eleven, Nick had gotten too big to play anymore and was sitting in one of the beanbags watching television.

"Hey there, Tuesday," Daddy said, when he saw me. "Wanna play?"

"Sure!" I said, and ran to him. I never passed up a chance to play the flying game.

Daddy, while lying on his back, bent his knees and pulled them in close to his body to get ready for me to climb on. Meanwhile, I leaned forward, resting my chest and belly on the soles of his feet. When he was sure my weight was balanced, he slowly extended his legs upward until they were perfectly straight.

High in the air, I closed my eyes and stretched my arms out as far as I dared, pretending to be an airplane, or a bird soaring in the sky. Daddy, at six feet seven inches tall, had the longest legs, but I wasn't afraid of being so high because I could sense his strength beneath me. And whenever I needed to, I could open my eyes and look down at his face for reassurance.

Daddy let me "fly" for a while, and then suddenly separated his legs, allowing me to slip off his feet and drop in front of him. Right before I fell, he caught me in midair. He never gave warning as to when he was going to do this, so each time my heart raced like crazy. But I trusted him enough that it didn't enter my mind that he might let me fall. And he never did.

After several turns each for Jimmy D. and me, Daddy's legs wore out and he announced the game was over. Tired from playing, we all cuddled up on the mattress to watch television. Just then

Mama poked her head in the doorway at the top of the stairs, and told us she was going into the living room to read for a while.

No one in the family but Mama ever spent much time in the living room. In contrast to the casual ranch style of the house, it was decorated formal Victorian. Heavy, tasseled, dark-green draperies hung to the floor over the picture window. In front of the window, proudly perched on cherry ball-and-claw feet, was a mauve tapestry sofa. In the middle of the room was Mama's marble-top cocktail table flanked by two Queen Anne chairs. On one wall was a drop-leaf table, on another, a cherry wood secretary desk with a *Gone with the Wind* lamp on top of it and a collection of ceramic Victorian figurines inside the hutch.

Some nights Mama sat in the living room all alone in one of the Queen Anne chairs, with a cup of hot tea or a glass of wine in her hand, gazing up at something seemingly out of her reach, a gentle yearning in her eyes. That night she curled up on the sofa with a book.

After a few hours of watching television, Daddy, the boys, and I were ready to go upstairs. On our way to bed, we passed by the living room and noticed Mama had fallen to sleep reading. It was not unusual for her to doze off on the sofa. Sometimes if she was sleeping well, Daddy let her stay there for the night.

He got a blanket from the linen closet in the hall and covered her up, and then he turned off the living room light. The boys went on to their beds, and Daddy walked with me to mine so he could tuck me in. "I'll be right down the hall if you need me," he said. But I wasn't afraid; I had no reason to be. Mama was on one side of me, and Daddy was on the other.

Through my sleepy haze, I heard Mama call out, "Audrey, are you okay?" Words I had grown accustomed to hearing because she still woke up often through the night thinking Audrey was calling for her.

"I'm coming!" yelled Mama. "I'll be right there!"

Then a loud cracking sound that bounced off every wall of the house brought me upright in my bed. The sound reminded me of the time I was at one of Nick's baseball games and a player broke a wooden bat against a ball.

Daddy and the boys came charging down the hallway, and I jumped up and joined them. Nobody said it, but I knew we were headed for the living room, where Mama was.

When we got there, we saw that the sofa, dimly lit by streetlights shining through the window, was empty. Without hesitation Daddy turned back and ran through the kitchen and down the dark stairs to the den. Nick flipped on the light to the stairway and he, Jimmy D. and I followed Daddy.

Mama was lying at the bottom of the stairs, her head and shoulders on the floor and the lower half of her body sprawled across the stairs. She was not moving and a small puddle of blood was near her mouth. Daddy rushed to her and felt around on her neck for a pulse, and then turned and ran back up the stairs, pushing us kids along in front of him. "Everyone in the living room," he said, and grabbed the phone receiver off the kitchen wall to call for help.

As soon as he hung up the phone, he rushed back to Mama's side. I watched from the top of the stairway as he got down on his knees. "Please God, not my Rosie!" he pleaded. "Don't you dare take my Rosie from me!" He looked up above him, and I could see the tears rolling down his face. "I can't make it without her!"

I knew he loved Mama, as much as a child my age could have known. I had heard him tell her practically every day and

I had seen it in his affection for her, which he openly displayed. But that night, I remember *feeling* how much he loved her, the power of his love and the depth. It was the first time I'd ever known my daddy to cry. He had always represented strength and safety to me. He was the one who chased the monsters away and held me when I was hurt. Seeing him in such a weak and desperate state shook me at the core of my sense of security. I began to tremble with fear.

Within minutes, an ambulance had arrived and its red lights were tracing around and around the living room walls. Daddy went next door and got Lana to come and stay with my brothers and me, so he could follow Mama to the hospital. Nick, Jimmy D., and I all sat on the sofa, unusually close to one another and still as statues. We watched out the window as the paramedics loaded our mama into the ambulance on a stretcher, not knowing whether or not we were ever going to see her again.

9

This is what happened: Our house was laid out such that one end of it was a mirror image of the other. The living room, kitchen and my room, which was originally intended to be a small den, were at one end, and two bedrooms and the bathroom were at the other. When you walked out of my parents' bedroom and took an immediate right, you were in the boys' room, which used to be Audrey's. When you walked out of the living room and took a right, you were at the top of the stairway leading to the den. Half asleep and thinking she was in her bedroom, Mama, in her frantic effort to get to what she thought was Audrey calling out to her, walked out of the living room and took a right, running full force into what she thought was Audrey's bedroom, but was actually the stairs to the den.

From her fall down the stairs, Mama suffered what Daddy called a frontal lobe brain concussion. She also bruised one shoulder and hip. The puddle of blood I had seen around her head was from a laceration down the side of her face that required several stitches. Daddy said she had most likely cut it on the sharp wooden corner of the bottom step.

Daddy spent every night at the hospital with her. He got his mother, Grandma Storm, to come from Nashville to stay at our house and take care of my brothers and me. Mama was in the hospital for just under a week, but it seemed like an eternity.

Finally the day she was to be released arrived. My brothers and I woke early, got cleaned up and helped Grandma Storm straighten the house. Then we all sat in the living room and waited for Mama to come home.

When we saw the station wagon pull into the driveway, we all ran out of the house, but Daddy stopped us in the yard and told us to go back inside and wait for them. We went in and sat on the sofa and watched from the picture window as he pulled Audrey's old wheelchair out of the back of the station wagon, unfolded it, lifted Mama from out of the car and lowered her into the chair.

It took them forever to make it up to the house, and when at last they were at the door, I was disappointed because the person Daddy wheeled inside was not my mama. The strange woman had a bandage on her left cheek where Mama had cut her face on the stairs and she resembled Mama, but this woman's head was larger and her eyes that glared into the empty space in front of her were much darker.

She didn't even look at my brothers and me when Daddy pushed her by us in the living room. That's when I knew it was definitely not Mama; she would never have ignored her kids, no matter how bad she felt. Daddy had obviously brought the wrong person home from the hospital by mistake and I told him so. But he kept insisting it was Mama, and he even went so far as to wheel the stranger into their bedroom and put her on Mama's side of the bed.

For the rest of that day, and the days immediately after Mama came home from the hospital, she spent most of her time sleeping. She only got up when she had to go to the bathroom. If she needed something from the kitchen, she had Daddy, or me, or one of the boys get it for her. This made me worried, but Daddy assured me it was a good thing because the doctor had said rest was the best way to heal a brain concussion.

During her second week home, she got out of her room more. Once in a while, she even stepped into the backyard to get some fresh air, or to watch my brothers and me as we played outside. But when she was out, she was careful to keep her distance from the neighbors. If by chance she saw one of them, she threw her hand up and waved, but she made sure to avert her eyes from theirs, as she tucked her cheek to her shoulder and hurried back into the house. Daddy told us she did this because she was ashamed of the scar on her face.

After Mama had been home from the hospital for a few weeks, she started insisting I be by her side at all times. "Stay in here with me, Tuesday," she said. "Sit down here on the floor beside my bed so I can see you."

I did as she asked, but it was hard for me to sit still for so long. After she fell asleep, I slipped out of the room to play with my brothers, only to have her call for me to return when she woke up. Out of frustration I asked Daddy why she only wanted me with her and not my brothers.

"I'm not sure, honey, but if I had to guess, I'd say maybe she's afraid something will happen to you, like it did to Audrey. Maybe she's more protective with you because you're a girl."

He then explained to me that the doctor had said head injuries like the one Mama had sometimes caused personality changes and therefore she might not act like herself for a while. But he assured me it was a temporary condition. His words satisfied me, and made me feel proud that I was so important to Mama.

It was late in the afternoon. Mama was sleeping and I was sitting on the floor by her bed, listening to the rest of the family as they moved about in other parts of the house.

Daddy stuck his head inside the doorway and said he was going grocery shopping, and that he was taking the boys with him.

I wanted to go too and I begged him to take me, but he told me it would be more helpful to him if I stayed home with Mama. He said he was going to stop and pick up some burgers on the way back and as a special reward he would get me a strawberry milkshake.

Soon I heard the door shut behind them and the house got quiet. Hours passed. The room grew darker and darker, until I had nothing to look at but the light from the alarm clock beside Mama's bed. I fixed my eyes on the glowing numbers and watched the minutes slowly flip away.

At seven thirty, she stirred. Suddenly she sat up and turned on the lamp beside her bed. When the light hit her face, I saw that it was red and bloated and her eyes had bags under them. Her hair was flat on one side and it stood up at the crown, like a windblown flame.

With dazed eyes, she searched out the room, seemingly confused and disoriented, as if she had forgotten where she was. When she spotted me sitting on the floor, she squinted to focus on my face and cocked her head, first to one side, then to the other, like she was trying to figure out the species of a creature she'd never seen before.

Then her deep woe registered and she sank back into her pillow and cried. "I want to sleep forever," she said. "Please God, let me sleep forever!"

She slung one of her arms over to the nightstand, knocking off a glass half-full of watered-down tea and groped around until she found a bottle of pills the doctor had prescribed to help her sleep. She propped herself on one elbow, twisted off the cap and poured the shiny, red capsules out into her palm. Blinking hard, she stretched open her swollen eyes to get a better look at the pills. She poked each one with her forefinger, then stuffed them back into the bottle and returned them to the nightstand.

She picked up the phone and dialed. Someone on the other end answered and Mama said into the receiver, "I just called to say good-bye. I can't take it anymore without Audrey, so I called to say good-bye and to tell you that none of you will have to worry about me ever again." Then she slammed the receiver down, and reached for the sleeping pills.

The phone rang almost immediately. "Tuesday, answer that," Mama said. "It's your Aunt Barbara. Tell her I don't want to talk to her. Tell her I'm going to swallow this bottle of sleeping pills. Answer the phone now and tell her what I said."

I picked up the phone and said, "Hello." Mama was right. It was Aunt Barbara, her sister.

"Tuesday, is that you?" she asked, sounding surprised to hear my voice. "Let me speak to your mother, honey."

I offered the receiver to Mama. She shook her head no. "She doesn't want to talk," I said to Aunt Barbara. "She's going to swallow her sleeping pills!"

"Where's your daddy?" Barbara asked.

"He's gone to the grocery store."

"Tuesday, what is your mother doing right now?"

"She's crying and holding the pills."

"Hand her the phone; tell her I want to speak to her. If she won't talk to me, you're going to have to run next door and get a neighbor for help, while I call an ambulance. Now tell her everything I just said."

I did as Aunt Barbara instructed. When I'd finished talking, Mama jerked the phone from my hand. As soon as she got the receiver to her ear, she said, "You don't know how it is to lose a child. You don't know, and you don't care. Why do you act like you do?"

Right about then, I heard the front door open. Daddy was home. He walked into the bedroom carrying a white fast-food sack in one hand and my strawberry milkshake in the other. "What's going on in here?" he asked as he handed the milkshake and food to me.

"Mama is going to swallow all her sleeping pills!" I said.

Daddy walked over and took the pills from her, and then turned to me. "Tuesday, run along to the kitchen and eat your supper with your brothers," he said. And I was happy to go.

tHE StRANGER IN MAMA'S CLotHES

10

It was Sunday morning, and Mama was still in bed. Daddy had gotten up early and driven to Nashville to go to church with Grandma Storm. I was at the kitchen table, in a morning daze, shoveling Rice Krispies into my mouth.

Nick was sitting across from me, slicing a banana over his cereal. "You look like you have popcorn balls in your cheeks," he said.

"Who, me?" I asked, glaring at the sunlight reflecting off the silver flecks in the linoleum tabletop.

He pointed the butter knife he had in his hand at Jimmy D., who was beside me. "No, him."

I looked at Jimmy D., his cheeks bulging with cereal. Milk was oozing out of his lips and running down his chin. "You *do* look like you have popcorn balls in your cheeks!"

Jimmy D. got tickled, and blew milk and bits of Rice Krispies through his mouth and nose onto Nick's face. I cracked up.

That's when I heard Mama calling out from her bedroom. "Tuesday!" she yelled in her gravelly morning voice. "Tuesday!" she called out again, this time more insistent. "Come here now!"

I put my spoon down beside my bowl of cereal, wiped the milk from my mouth on the front of my pajamas and hurried down the hall to her bedroom.

When I got there, she was sitting up in the bed. She had just woken from a hard sleep. I could tell from the deep creases in the side of her face.

I bounced up to her and sat down. "What do you want, Mama?"

"I don't know what you're so happy about, young lady, because you're in big trouble!"

Springing up, I started back-pedaling and searching my memory for something I might have done to upset her. I couldn't remember doing any of the usual things that got me into trouble, like running in the house, or fighting with my brothers and my school grades were good. But it was obvious she was mad about something. I could see the rage in her face, hear it in her voice.

I stood before her, nervous, and suddenly cold from the wet spot where I'd wiped milk on my pajamas. "Why, Mama, what did I do wrong?"

"Don't play dumb with me, girl! You know exactly what you did!" she said in a growly tone she had never used with me before. "As punishment I want you to stand in the hallway with your face to the wall." From her bed, she pointed to an area between two doorways right outside her room. "Stay there until I say you can move."

While I stood with my face to the wall, I continued to try to figure out what mysterious bad thing I had done. And all I could come up with was the time I'd let Audrey chew my bubble-gum. I knew if Mama found out there was a possibility I'd given Audrey the flu that killed her, she would certainly be mad. But there was no way she could have found out, unless Audrey had told her before she died.

Suddenly Mama leaped from her bed and ran into the hallway where I was. She grabbed me by both of my shoulders and spun me around, facing her. "Why did it have to be my angel?" she screamed. "Why *Audrey?*"

"I don't know, Mama," I screamed back at her. "I don't *know!*"

She shook me back and forth. "Tell me! Tell me why, why, Tuesday, why?"

It was the last time she ever said my name.

11

I thought my face to the wall punishment would last only a few minutes and then I would go back into the kitchen and finish my breakfast. But a few minutes turned to hours and I ended up staying there for the rest of the day, until it was time for me to go to bed.

The next day the radical change in Mama's attitude toward me continued. She went from asking me to stay by her side, in a protective way, to demanding I be within her sight at all times, as if she didn't trust me. And she no longer wanted me close to her, by her bed, but rather in the hallway outside her room, positioned so she could watch me.

She wouldn't tell me why she was angry. She would say only that I had done something so horrible she couldn't even bear to talk about it and that I needed to be punished for what I'd done. She said the punishment she had chosen was for me to stand with my face turned to the wall in the hall outside her bedroom door and that I was not to speak unless she asked me a question.

As soon as I got up every morning, she ordered me to stand in the same place, in the same position and that's where I remained until it was time to go to bed. I ate my meals in the hall. If I had to go to the bathroom, I asked for permission and she went with me. When she felt well enough to venture out of her bed and do a few things around the house, she took me with her. She said she had to make sure I didn't do anything else.

Once, Nick passed by me on his way to the bathroom and asked me what I was doing standing there. "I don't know," I told him. "Mama said I did something bad, but I can't remember what it was and she won't tell me."

"Leave her alone," Mama shouted from her bedroom when she saw us talking. "She's being punished."

Nick didn't try to challenge her. Since her accident, he and Jimmy D. had trod softly around her and indulged her every whim, no matter how outrageous. I was afraid to say anything too, afraid she would lash out at me again and ask more questions about Audrey, questions I couldn't answer.

With each passing day, Mama isolated me from my brothers more and more. It got to where whenever one of them passed by me in the hallway, they promptly turned away, like they were afraid if they looked too long, or got too close they might catch whatever it was I had that made me different, made me bad.

Somehow they were able to separate the way she treated me from the world they lived in with her. Every now and then, I caught Jimmy D. staring at me with something resembling pity in his eyes. It was a far-removed emotion, though, the way one might look at a poster of a starving third-world child. Like he felt sad and guilty to see my suffering, but there was nothing he could do about it. I sensed he wanted to help me, but his sympathy and good intentions were always overshadowed both by his fear of Mama and his great love for her.

Staring at the blank wall, I listened to my brothers' distant voices as they played, straining to hear fragments of their conversations so I could in some way remain a part of their lives. I wanted desperately to be near them, but it was impossible because now I wasn't allowed speak to them, or even look their way. Mama had become adamant about this rule. She warned us—no communication at all, and we knew she meant it. We could see it in her eyes; if we disobeyed her there would be fiery hell to pay.

12

When it was time for me to return to school in September, I was sure my life would get back to normal. But it didn't. Every day, as soon as I got home, Mama met me at the door and ordered me to go to my usual spot outside her bedroom and stand with my face to the wall.

One afternoon, she decided she would get up and prepare a fried chicken supper for the family. She had me follow her to the kitchen and stand behind her, across the room, but still facing the wall.

When I was sure she was busy at the stove, I took a chance and turned around so I could see her. I knew I'd be in trouble if she caught me, but I loved watching her cook. To me, it was like wizardry when she lifted the lids from the pans and the puffs of steam rose. She could perform wondrous acts in the kitchen, like turn grease into gravy, or put a liquid batter in the oven and minutes later, pull out a cake.

She looked good that day, almost like she'd looked before her accident. She had changed out of her gown into snug black pants and a simple, peach button-down blouse that she'd tied up in a high knot around her waist. She could get by with dressing a bit on the sexy side, because even after four kids, she had kept her tiny waist and her full, taut bottom.

Daddy said she had been built even better when they first starting dating. "I could put my hands completely around her waist with room to spare," he'd once said, proudly, as he formed a circle in the air with his long fingers. "I was the envy of every man in town. Every guy I knew wanted to go out with Rosie, but she picked me."

The air in the tiny kitchen was dense with steam and rich with the scent of Mama's cooking. I inhaled deeply and took in her every movement. She jabbed a chicken leg with a fork, suspended it above the frying pan to allow some of the grease to drain, and then transferred it onto a plate lined with paper towels.

She made the best fried chicken ever. The batter was super crunchy, with a hint of sweetness and it had a spicy kick to it. Daddy claimed it was the best in Spring Hill, if not in the entire state of Tennessee. She used a family recipe passed down from her grandmother to her mother, to her, a recipe so sacred, so secret, no one had ever even written it down. She'd let me help her make chicken before and I knew she dipped it in buttermilk and double-battered it, but even I didn't know the secret spices. She had promised to tell me someday.

Piece by piece, she pulled all the fried chicken from the pan and then scraped the crusty bits of batter that had stuck to the bottom, preparing to make the gravy. She scooped some flour out of a canister and sprinkled it into the pan and the hot grease hissed. When she added cold milk, it purred.

While the gravy simmered, she whipped up some cornbread batter and then dumped it into a cast-iron skillet.

As she was bending over to put the cornbread into the oven to bake, something, possibly a small sound, or maybe the curious, uneasy sensation you get when you think someone is watching you, made her look back.

Quickly I turned my face to the wall again. But it was too late; I had already been caught. I heard the oven door slam and in the next instant, felt the hair on one side of my head being pulled. I saw the brown specks in the floor rushing toward me and then my cheek smacked hard against cold linoleum.

"Weren't you supposed to have your face turned to the wall?" she asked.

I didn't answer her at first; I was too stunned from the fall. But when she started for me again, I somehow found the words. "Yes, Mama! Yes!"

She reached down and grabbed me by the hair again, this time with both her hands, one on each side of my head, and lifted me up from the floor. I could hear my scalp crunching as she drew me in to her, close, until my nose was almost touching hers, until I could feel her breath, hot and moist on my skin. "Well, then, why were you watching me?"

"I love you, Mama!" I cried "Please don't be mad at me anymore!"

"Since you like watching me so much, do it now!" she screamed. The veins in her temple turned purple and bulged, as if they might burst at any minute.

As she held me there in front of her, with my face less than an inch from hers, my legs dangling, I looked into her amber eyes and they reminded me of the eyes of a lioness. I was so scared I began to shake all over. "Let me down!" I pleaded. "I'm sorry, Mama, I won't do it again!"

She dropped me to the floor. "You're damn right, you won't do it again." she said, plucking strands of my hair from between her fingers.

She stood and stared at me for a minute and then said, "Do you want to know what you *really* did wrong?" Her voice was husky, and her jaw was clenched so tight she had to squeeze the words through her teeth. "You were born, that's what!"

She kicked me in the side and a wave of nausea coursed through me. When she pulled her leg back to kick me again, I coiled into a ball, tucking my head and knees in to my chest and tensing all my muscles.

She delivered the blow. "On top of that, you were born ugly!" She kicked me again and screamed, "Go away! Why won't you just go away?"

With every thrust of her foot, my body rocked and then slid, rocked and slid across the kitchen, inches at a time. Finally my back hit the table, toppling a bowl of wax fruit onto the floor. Apples, pears and bananas bounced all around me, sending hollow echoes through the room.

All of a sudden, she spun around on one heel and marched toward the back door. I pulled my body in tight, into the hardest ball I could manage, and watched, as in a single, swift motion she lifted the flyswatter from its hook by the door, and with the wire handle first, reared it behind her head and made a running lunge for me.

Instinctively I brought my hands up to protect my face. The wire sliced across my forearms. I pushed one hand forward to block the next blow, leaving part of my face exposed. The wire hit my mouth and I screamed. As if my screaming had enraged her even more, she broke into a barrage of blows. The flyswatter came at me from every direction, landing on my shoulders, back and arms. I rolled from side to side, trying to find some padding to put between me and the wire, but I was a skinny kid and no matter where it landed, it hit bone.

Finally the blows tapered off. She gave the last two everything she had left. "I hate you!" She spat the words as if they tasted bitter on her tongue. "I wish you'd never been born! If you'd never been born my angel would still be alive!"

There it was—the reason for her anger toward me. I uncovered my eyes. "What?" I asked.

She stood over me looking at the flyswatter in her hand— now bent in half—as if she didn't know how it had gotten there. "You heard me. Now get out of my sight!" she yelled. "Go to bed…and stay there until I say you can get up!"

Scrambling to my knees, I started scooting across the kitchen towards my bedroom. As I bent forward, I felt something wet and warm oozing through the crevice of my lips. A red drop splattered the floor in front of me. I wiped it up with my hand and caught another before it landed. When I made it to my room, I stood and ran to my bed and got in. Mama slammed the door shut behind me.

With my fingers I gently explored the tender, puffy tissue of my mouth until I found the source of the blood, a small slit in the fleshy part of my upper lip. I wiped my face and chin on the inside of my shirt collar until the bleeding stopped.

As I lay there, I tried not to think about what had happened in the kitchen. But every time I shut my eyes to sleep my mind deceived me. Mama's angry face and the sound of the wire thrashing against my bones flashed through my head over and over like scenes from a horror movie.

I tried to reason it away, to convince myself that she was only angry and hadn't meant it when she said she hated me.

Since the accident, she was more easily riled. I had grown accustomed—we'd all grown accustomed—to her frequent fits. I calmed down by deciding her rage had spurned her hateful words, not her heart, and that she would never say such mean things to me again.

Had it not been for what she said, I may have stored the entire incident away somewhere deep in my subconscious, unprocessed. With time, it may have even faded into history. But what she said changed everything. It was proof she thought I was the one to blame for Audrey's death and the reason why she'd been punishing me.

I defended myself, to myself. *I wasn't the only one in the house who had the flu. How is she so sure it was my fault Audrey got sick? Does she know about the bubble-gum? If she does, how did she find out? Did she see it on the nightstand and figure it out for herself? Or did Audrey rat on me before she died?*

I tossed and turned in bed. *None of it matters anyway because even if I did kill Audrey, it wasn't on purpose. I didn't know for sure I had the flu. When Mama gets over her anger and pain, she will realize the truth and forgive me, like she did with Jacque. But what is the truth? Is the truth that I wanted Audrey dead and then made it happen? That whether I meant to or not, it's still because of me that she's gone?*

Mama called out that supper was ready and the boys ran past my room on their way to the kitchen. I heard their chairs drag across the floor as they sat at the table. Daddy would not be eating with the family, because he was working late. His job as coach of the Spring Hill High School football team often called him away at night to attend ball practices and games.

Soon I heard forks scraping against plates and ice rattling around in glasses, as Mama and the boys ate their supper. I pictured the platter of fried chicken piled high with crispy wings, thighs, and breasts glistening with salt and grease, and the mound of mashed potatoes with creamy milk gravy. My stomach ached and rumbled, begging for food.

To get my mind off of eating, I looked around my room, and was suddenly struck by how empty it had become. For the past couple of weeks, since Mama had become mad at me, I had noticed my toys had begun to disappear. My Barbie dolls were the first to go, then one by one my troll collection.

As the room darkened, my eyes were drawn to the few glints of sun escaping the blinds of the window. I stared at the slivers of light and watched them grow dim and then finally disappear. Gradually the smell of Mama's fried chicken was gone too and I knew with it went my chances of getting anything to eat.

In the dark, I listened to all the usual sounds the family made in the evenings: Mama gathering and washing the supper dishes, my brothers scuffling around in their bedroom. Before long, I heard Mama coming up the hallway. I could always recognize the cadence of her walk—soft, but fast and deliberate. *She's coming to tell me she's sorry.*

She stopped in front of my bedroom. As she opened the door, the light from the hall surrounded her, marking the familiar curves of her silhouette. Without making a sound, she stood there in the doorway, her face shadowed by the dark room in front of her. For those few seconds, with the pure optimism only a child could have, my heart held on to the possibility that she hadn't meant what she'd said in the kitchen, that she had come to soothe my wounds.

"I'm sorry, Mama," I said. "Can I get up now? I'm hungry."

She pulled a towel from the linen closet in the hallway and tossed it to me. "Here, take this and clean your face," she said.

"Please, Mama," I cried out to her. "Please don't be mad anymore. I love you!"

She turned and left, pulling the door to behind her. The darkness swallowed her up, along with all the light, all but one thin line that shone through the crack under the door. In that slice of light, I watched her shadow skim across the floor until it was gone.

Soon, she and the boys settled in for the night in front of the television set in her bedroom. Crying, I listened to the distant drone of their voices, broken by occasional bursts of laughter, until I eventually drifted off to sleep.

13

I awoke to the sound of the front door opening. My heart leaped. *Daddy's home!*

Nick and Jimmy D. met him as soon as he came in the house. Jimmy D. said in a low, urgent voice, "Tuesday did something bad again and Mama spanked her really hard this time."

I heard Daddy walking up the hallway, taking his usual long strides. The door to my bedroom opened. I kept my eyes shut, but I was aware of the light from the hall shining across my face. Through cracked eyelids, I watched him walk in and turn in the direction of my bed.

As he approached me, I pretended like I was asleep. I wanted to appear innocent, like a sleeping angel, not an evil killer. I wanted him to see the cut on my lip and the bloody towel by my head and to feel sorry for me. I wanted him to get mad at Mama for hurting me, plenty mad. Mad enough to jerk her up from bed and demand an explanation.

He knelt on the floor beside me and brushed the hair away from my face. I winced when his thumb found a fresh knot on my forehead that I hadn't been aware of. "Honey, you awake?" he whispered.

I couldn't pretend any longer. I sprang up, wrapped my arms around his neck and buried my face into his shoulder, inhaling the sweet, spicy scent of his cologne.

"Just wanted to say good night," he said.

I told him what had happened earlier with Mama and about what she had said.

He held me in his arms to comfort me. "Try not to pay much attention when your mama says crazy things like that," he said. "She hasn't been in her right mind since the accident."

He held me a few minutes longer and promised me he would have a talk with her.

"It's late, honey; time to go to sleep," he said, laying me down. "I'll come back and see you in the morning."

As he had promised, he went to Mama about my injuries. He didn't jerk her out of bed like I had hoped, but they did have an argument. I could hear curse words being thrown back and forth between them. I got up and tiptoed across the room to the door so I could better hear what they were saying.

"How did Tuesday get the big bump on her head?" Daddy asked.

"She defied me...and so I spanked her." Mama said, like it was no big deal.

"And the cut on her lip?"

"I don't know. She must have hit it on something. You've seen how she flinches and dodges me when I'm trying to discipline her."

"What could she have cut it on?"

"What are you trying to insinuate? You have no idea what happened because you weren't here. You're never here to help with the kids anymore, so stay out of it!"

"Why are you harder on her than the other kids?" Daddy fired back.

"I'm *not* harder on her!" she shouted. "And I'm not going to sit here and let you accuse me of being a bad mother."

I heard the mattress springs squeak, signaling that Mama was getting up, and then she came storming down the hall. I raced back to my bed before she got to my door. When she passed by, I shuddered because I was afraid she might attack me again. But more than anything else, I was afraid Daddy would one day find out what I had done and turn against me too.

14

Mama's anger toward me continued to increase with each passing day. Her sudden verbal and physical attacks became more frequent and severe and more unpredictable, bursting upon her from out of nowhere, for no apparent reason.

Whenever she lost it with me, she always said the same things she had said that first time in the kitchen—that it was my fault Audrey was dead, and she hated me because I'd been born and because I was ugly.

Up until that point in my life, I had never given much thought to how I looked. Daddy had always told me I was beautiful and so had Mama before she got mad at me. But now after hearing her say over and over that I was ugly, I was beginning to get the message that the way she saw me had changed and to realize my looks were something important, if not essential, to her loving me.

She valued beauty above all else, because in her life, beauty had brought her many good things. "I was the prettiest and most popular girl in my school," she'd boasted. "I was homecoming queen and head cheerleader at the same time. I had my pick of boys!"

Still even after I had figured out I needed to be beautiful to gain her love and acceptance, I didn't have the slightest clue how to make it happen. Whenever I got the chance, I examined my face in the mirror and compared my features to those of my siblings. I couldn't understand how it was that I was ugly and they were not when we so closely resembled one another. Why Mama thought they were cute, but not me. These thoughts burdened both my mind and my heart.

One afternoon, I was standing in my usual place in the hall when Mama came up and dangled an old dishcloth in front of me. "Put this over your face," she said.

At first I went blank. Then I remembered she had made my brothers and me wear similar masks over our faces when we had the flu to shield Audrey from germs. *But I'm not sick. Why does she want me to wear a mask now?*

She explained how she was tired of "looking at my ugly face" and that she was certain Daddy and the boys were too.

Baffled, I looked at her, then at the mask, then at her again.

"Here, I'll do it for you," she said. She folded the cloth into a triangle, wrapped it around my face and tied it in a tight knot at the base of my head. "Now, that's better," she said, stepping back.

She told me I was to put the mask on as soon as I got in from school every day, wear it while I did my chores and take it off only when I went to school. To make my life easier, I always did whatever she said, even if it didn't make any sense. So I put the mask on every afternoon right after school and on the weekends I wore it all day.

I hated the mask. It was hot and uncomfortable, and it smashed my nose flat, which sometimes gave me a panicky feeling, like I was smothering. It was also embarrassing and degrading when I wore it around Daddy and my brothers. But after having it on every day for about a month, I got used to it and after a while, a weird thing happened—I became attached to it. Dependent on it, in the same way a baby is dependent on a security blanket. I took comfort in the distinct, heady odor it had acquired and the protective shield it put between Mama's critical eyes and the imperfections of my face. Without it I felt vulnerable and exposed.

15

"Hon, run and get us a bottle of Southern Comfort from the liquor store," Mama said to Daddy in her most seductive voice. "After we get the kids to sleep, we'll have a few drinks and play cards in our room tonight."

Daddy eagerly responded to her invitation with a mischievous grin and just like that he was out the door headed for the liquor store.

According to Mama, it was not "Southern proper" for a lady to be seen at a liquor store, so whenever she was in the mood for alcohol, she had no choice but to ask Daddy to buy it for her. You could always tell when she wanted some, because she would suddenly sweeten up to him and start talking sexy.

Daddy openly proclaimed his attraction to Mama and his good fortune that she had agreed to marry him. He had a favorite black and white photograph he kept in his wallet of the two of them when they first started dating. He liked to pull it out whenever he reminisced about their first days together. In it Mama had on a tea-length, bustier dress, classic pumps and a single string of pearls. Daddy, at least a foot and a half taller, stood behind her with his hands wrapped around her tiny waist he loved so much. He was wearing an ill-fitting suit and an I-just-won-the-big-prize grin on his face. He had the same dazed look he always had whenever he was around her, like he was anesthetized by her potent pheromones, causing everything around him to be fuzzy, unclear.

I could tell by the things I had heard Mama say to Daddy when they argued that she thought he was just this side of ugly. Like any young girl, I thought my daddy was the handsomest man in the world. He was well-groomed and dressed neatly and he wore his dark-blonde hair in a clean flattop. He was a big man, tall, broad and square-framed, and as is the case with many men of significant size, his features were large, almost giant-like. His face was also badly scarred with deep pockmarks from the severe acne he had in his youth. Sometimes when she was mad, Mama called him pit face and I felt sorry for him then.

Once I heard her tell him had she not been a divorcee with a crippled daughter, she would have landed a better man, one who could have provided her with all she desired and deserved. Instead she had to "settle," as she put it, for Daddy, a high school teacher with a meager income. If you looked close at Daddy's favorite picture of the two of them, you could see her smile was plastic, like the smile on a doll's face and she had a mad-at-the-world look deep in her eyes. She was mad because she ended up with the goofy giant instead of the wealthy prince.

Daddy made it back from the liquor store in record time. Mama took her Southern Comfort into the bedroom and he joined her, shutting the door behind them.

More times than not, when they went into their room to "play cards," Mama got drunk on her alcohol, became angry about something that went on in the bedroom and came bolting out. When this happened, they typically argued all night long, ruining any chance for Daddy to get lucky. Other nights the door would remain shut and the "card game" would go on as planned. It was the slim possibility and titillating uncertainty that kept him falling for the same routine, time after time.

On this night I heard them arguing for a while before Mama came out stomping down the hallway, Daddy right behind her. I watched from my bed as she went into the bathroom and dug through the dirty laundry basket until she found the shirt he'd worn to work that day. While he was at the liquor store, I'd seen her put some of her lipstick on the same shirt and had wondered why she was doing it.

"This time I have proof you're screwing around," she said, holding the tainted shirt in front of his face.

Since her accident, she had convinced herself Daddy was having an affair and she interrogated him about it practically every day. Her paranoia had progressed to the point where she had him strip off all his clothes as soon as he walked in the door from work. Then she spent hours in the bathroom, sniffing every inch of them—even the crotches of his underwear—for traces of perfume and inspecting them, thread by thread, for makeup. She failed to find anything incriminating on his clothing, and this became a great source of frustration for her, because she was sure he was sleeping with someone.

"What the hell are you talking about, Rose?" Daddy asked, genuinely bewildered.

"Take a look for yourself, you bastard, and *you* tell *me*." She pushed the shirt with the "evidence" on it closer to his eyes. "There's lipstick all over your collar. Don't you think I know lipstick when I see it?"

Daddy took the shirt from her and examined it closely. He was becoming more and more confused by the minute; you could see it in his face. "I don't know how this—whatever it is—got on my shirt, but I am not having an affair."

"Who is she, Nick?"

"There is no one!" Daddy shouted, as he walked away.

Mama followed behind him, pounding at his back with both her fists. "Don't you walk away from me you son of a bitch!"

"Damn it, Rose, get off me! Leave me alone!"

"How dare you? How dare you cheat on me? Any man would kill to have me—any man!"

16

The months passed, with every sunrise bringing the possibility that Mama wouldn't be mad at me anymore. But every evening the sun set on her rage and hateful words. Until she got better, all I had was Daddy. He had become the center of my existence, my only hope.

In the morning, before he left for work and I, for school, he always came to my bed and held me close. He told me how pretty he thought I was, how special. It was for these snippets of his affection that I now lived.

On the weekends, after he had given me my morning kiss, he sometimes prepared a big Southern-style breakfast for the family: fried or scrambled eggs, sausage patties, biscuits and gravy, and either grits or hash browns, sometimes both.

He loved big breakfasts and being in the kitchen early in the morning. He loved how the sunlight sifted through the oak tree by the window casting lacy shadows on the walls that danced around the room when the wind blew. Even under dour circumstances, he always managed to find some small reason to be joyful when he got up, to inspire him to whistle merrily as he rolled out the biscuit dough and scrambled up the eggs, the coffee percolating in the background. Like when I was six, and an unexpected early spring snow spread a glistening white blanket over the backyard. He was so excited he woke everyone in the family to see it.

He wanted to share his breakfasts with Mama and the boys, but they were late risers and often grumpy upon awakening, and without appetite. Even though he tried, he sometimes couldn't get them out of bed at all to eat what he had prepared. On these mornings, he would sit at the kitchen table in silence and eat his breakfast all alone. My heart sank for him then and I often wondered what he was thinking. His life couldn't have been the one he had imagined for himself, growing up as he did in a loving, nurturing family that began each day with hugs, gleeful chatter, and a hearty breakfast together. In bed, alone and hungry, there were many mornings when I listened to his movements in the kitchen, his whistling, and wished he would come get me and ask me to eat with him, but he never did.

One chilly, February morning, I squirmed around in my bed as he got ready for work. I could hardly wait for him to finish and come to see me. I had monitored his morning routine so many times I had his every movement memorized. I listened as he stepped out onto the front porch to get the paper, and then retreat into the bathroom to read it while he sat on the toilet. Then he took his shower. Afterward, he opened the door to let the steam out and a warm, soapy smell drifted down the hall and into my room.

When I heard him filling the sink, I knew it meant he was getting ready to shave. I could hear the splashing of water as he dipped the razor in, and then the tap, tap, tap of it on the side of the sink. When he finished, he slapped his face with aftershave and then headed for the bedroom to get dressed. As soon as I heard him pick up his keys and loose change from the nightstand, I became eager, because I knew what was next.

Finally he came to my bed, sat on the edge and said in his hushed, morning voice, "Hold on a little longer, honey." Then he bent over me, touched his lips to my cheek and told me he loved me. "I'll make her stop, I promise," he said. "Give me some more time."

Even at my young age, I had already learned how to read him through the many expressions of his face. When he was happy, his eyes twinkled. When he was angry or worried, he furrowed his brow. That morning, as the sun cast a hazy light across his face, his eyes drooped with sadness and there were dark circles of worry around them.

"Okay, Daddy," I said, because I believed him. He was all I had to believe in.

He picked up one of my arms and began rubbing it, smoothing out the scraggly blonde hairs. "I'm sorry your mama is always mad at you."

"Why is she mad at me?" I asked, pretending like I didn't know. "What did I do?"

"You didn't do anything, honey." He stopped rubbing my arm and turned his head away from me, as if to collect his thoughts. "It's just that she's still upset about Audrey."

Then he changed the subject and with it, the timbre of his voice. "How would you like to go to Nashville to visit Grandma Storm for a while this summer?"

I loved Grandma Storm, and I hardly ever got to see her. "Stay at her house all night?" I asked, barely able to contain myself.

"Sure, maybe for several nights."

I threw my arms around his neck. His cheeks were smooth, clean of the scratchy whiskers he often had at night.

Then a thought quelled my excitement. I pulled away from his embrace and eyed him in disbelief. "Mama won't let me go."

"Yes, she will. I might have to work on her, but she'll let you."

"Please, Daddy," I begged. "Please take me to Grandma's house right now!"

He chuckled. "No, you have to finish out the school year first. And I'll have to talk it over with Grandma Storm to make sure it's okay."

He gave me my morning kiss good-bye and left for work. I savored the smell of his Old Spice for as long as I could after he was gone.

17

In June, as he had promised, Daddy made the arrangements for me to visit Grandma Storm at her house in Nashville. He got me out of bed early one Saturday morning before anyone else in the family awoke, threw my clothes in a brown paper bag and drove me there.

Within half an hour, we were at Grandma's. As the station wagon pulled up her bumpy, gravel driveway, I marveled at all the flowers in full bloom in her front yard. There were pink petunias in a circular bed around a dogwood tree and three side-by-side symmetrical islands of red geraniums, one with a birdbath in the center. Red and white peonies lined the stone pathway leading to the front porch and roses of every color climbed trellises close to the house. I rolled down the car window and stuck my face out, breathing in the fragrant air.

Daddy parked the car and together we made our way to Grandma Storm's front door. He carried the paper bag with my clothes in it in one hand and pulled me along behind him with the other. We took a shortcut, hurrying across a patch of dewy grass between the house and the driveway and my feet slid around on my rubber flip-flops as I struggled to keep up with him.

The door to Grandma's house was open, as it always was to family, and we went right inside without even knocking.

The furniture in her living room was grand and large scale and out of proportion with her tiny, cottage-like home. That's because she'd once lived in a big plantation house that had been destroyed by fire in the early 1900s. The living room furniture, including a baby grand piano, was practically all she had been able to salvage.

When the tragedy struck, Grandma refused to leave what was left of her home, and the flower garden that had taken her years to perfect. She and my grandfather a successful lawyer, decided to rebuild on the same property and, as much as they possibly could, put everything back the way it had been before the fire.

That was their intention, but before they could get started, the Great Depression closed in and my grandfather became ill, dying in his fifties of complications from diabetes. Without his income to finance the project, Grandma had to settle for much less. The garage, which was the only part of the house spared by the fire, was sectioned off into two parts to become the den and kitchen of the new house. The living and dining rooms, and two bedrooms, were added on to complete it.

Daddy's older sister, Macy, was seated at the kitchen table reading the newspaper. She had recently divorced her husband and moved in with Grandma Storm until she got back on her feet. When we entered the room, she peered up over her bifocals and smiled pleased to see we had arrived.

We found Grandma busy at the stove making breakfast. Even at the early hour, she was already dressed in a bright blue floral smock and her hair was neatly pinned up in a twisted bun. As soon as she heard us come in, she stopped what she was doing and wiped her hands on the dish towel draped across her shoulder. "Come here!" she said, spreading her arms wide and thrusting them high into the air.

I ran to her and hugged her around the hips, pushing my face into her soft, warm belly. She smelled like a mixture of bacon and the lingering scent of soap from her morning bath.

"Did you bring a dress for church in the morning?" she asked.

I looked to Daddy for the answer.

"She doesn't have a dress suitable for church, Mom," he said in an apologetic tone.

Grandma patted me on my back. "That's alright," she said. "We'll just have to go shopping and get you one tonight, won't we?"

The kitchen table was set for four. Four large Blue Willow plates were waiting to be filled with bacon, grits and eggs made to order. Four blue, cut-glass goblets were filled with orange juice. Beside each plate was a second smaller plate with two pieces of buttered toast sliced in half diagonally and to the right of the toast, a pink grapefruit half in a bowl.

Grandma made our eggs and we sat to eat right away. I gobbled down two fried eggs, two pieces of toast with apple jelly, three slices of bacon and a heaping pile of buttery grits. I even ate my grapefruit, which I didn't know I liked. It tasted good with sugar sprinkled on top.

Daddy inhaled his breakfast too, and then told Grandma he had to get home to mow the grass. He got up from the table, bent down and gave me a hug and a kiss, and then made a quick exit. I panicked and followed him to the door and watched from a window as he backed the station wagon out of the drive and disappeared down the road.

Later in the day, after going through my bag of clothes and discovering I hadn't brought much of anything with me, Aunt Macy drove me to JC Penney's to shop for an outfit for me to wear to church on Sunday.

She helped me select a pale yellow dress with white pin dots. To go with the dress, we picked out white ankle socks trimmed in lace, and glossy black patent leather shoes. "This will get you started," Aunt Macy said. "I have some fabric remnants at home, and next week, I'll get my sewing machine out and whip you up a few more church dresses and maybe some shorts to play in."

All the shopping made us hungry. On the way back home, we stopped at Shoney's Restaurant to grab a bite to eat. Aunt Macy was shocked when I wolfed down two hamburgers and an order of fries. She laughed at me when I would, from time to time, stop eating and squeal with delight. I couldn't help it; I was that happy.

Sunday we attended the morning service at the Trinity Presbyterian Church, located a few blocks from Grandma's house. When we got close to the entrance to the church, I looked up at the towering steeple with its soaring cross piercing the sky and was instantly aware that I was a part of something huge, something important. Once we were inside, I became mesmerized by all the different colors in the stained-glass windows surrounding me.

Grandma and Aunt Macy were not fanatics about religion, but they were firm in their belief of God and their faith was an often-silent, but ever-present, part of their lives.

Aunt Macy read the Bible every night before she went to bed and sometimes in the morning before she left for work. I asked her once why it was taking her so long to finish it and she told me she would never be finished with the Bible, because as soon as she reached the last page, she planned to go right back to the first one and start all over again. "I have read it three times already, from cover to cover," she said. "And every time I've learned something new."

It was Grandma who first introduced me to God. I took comfort when she told me a powerful, all-knowing being was watching over me and that He had control over everything, even Mama. It gave me hope my situation at home might change for the better. She taught me how to pray. She told me to remember to say grace before each meal and to offer my thanks to God and Jesus at night before I went to sleep. She urged me not to let a single day pass without thanking Him for all his wonderful blessings and asking Him to forgive me for anything bad I might have done during the day. "He will always be there for you to get you through the hard times. All you have to do is ask for His help," she said. "He has a plan for each and every one of us on earth and all things, both bad and good, happen for a reason."

Hearing this made me wonder what my special purpose was in life and the reason for all the terrible things happening to me at home.

During the day, while Aunt Macy was at work. I was content to play by myself while Grandma watched soap operas and puttered around the house. My favorite game was "secretary." I invented it to emulate Aunt Macy at her job. I dressed up in her clothes and even found an old typewriter on which I pretended to type important work documents.

Other days I went outside and made dandelion necklaces or mud pies. For a special treat, when it was extra hot, Grandma got a large washtub from the shed and filled it with water and soapsuds for me to play in. Sometimes she would spray me with the garden hose. I played all day until the sun went down and at night I caught fireflies and put them in Mason jars, until Grandma made me come inside.

On the weekends, we often went to Centennial Park for a picnic where I fed the ducks, or to the Parthenon to look at the Greek statues, or to the theater to see the latest Disney movie. At home, we played croquet and badminton in the huge yard that had once been a tennis court. Other times, we went to put fresh flowers on my grandfather's grave. Grandma was downhearted and reserved on those days.

She liked to talk about her life before the fire when money was plentiful and she and my grandfather hosted elaborate dinner parties. She reminisced about the old days with a lilt in her voice and glitter in her eyes.

Because she had also lived during the Depression, she talked about those days too. But whenever she told me about how her life was then, her voice took on a somber tone. It was during this deprived period that she first began to save everything that could possibly be of any use at a later date. Her kitchen drawers were stuffed with rubber bands and neatly folded sheets of crumpled tin foil. The cabinets were crammed full of empty butter tubs that toppled out on your head when you opened the doors.

My life at Grandma's house was the opposite of the one I knew at home. I ate anything I wanted, anytime I was hungry. I went to the bathroom whenever I needed to. I wore ribbons in my hair and took bubble baths. Grandma and Aunt Macy bought me clothes and toys. They lavished me with love and affection and I was the center of their life.

When I was there, I was not ugly. In fact, they were forever going on and on about how cute I was to everybody they knew. They dressed me up and took countless pictures, posing me in front of the flowers in Grandma's garden, at the park feeding the ducks and sitting on the piano. All this made me question what Mama had said about the way I looked. I spent hours in front of the mirror analyzing every curve of my face and examining all the pictures Grandma and Aunt Macy had taken of me, wondering how it could be they saw something completely different than Mama.

Grandma had a burgundy leather photo album where she kept all the pictures she had taken of her grandkids. She got it out one day, pulled out a photograph, and handed it to me. "That's you, sweetie, when you were about four months old," she said, pointing to a pale, smidgen of a creature with a puff of cottony hair.

I stared at the photograph long and hard. "Grandma, do you think I'm ugly?"

"Heavens, no!" she said, without pause. "You're beautiful, you've always been beautiful." She took my face into her hands, squeezing my cheeks together till my mouth puckered and gave me a firm kiss on the top of the head. "Now quit talking nonsense."

I didn't know how much Grandma and Aunt Macy knew about my situation at home. They never brought up Mama to me and they were careful to avoid the subject of her accident. But I suspected they discussed these things when I was not around, because they often spoke in low voices that stopped promptly whenever I entered the room.

They never said anything to me about the bruises all over my body, or the scars that peppered my hairline. But once, when Grandma was helping me with my bath, tears welled in her eyes. "Honey, you barely have enough hair to cover your head," she said, and I detected a faint sob in her voice.

It didn't occur to me to tell her or Aunt Macy about the horrible things Mama had said and done to me. I didn't think much about it while I was there, or worry over what awaited me when I returned home. I was too full of joy, wallowing in a world filled with love, a place where I was welcome and cherished, to be bothered by what lay ahead.

Unlike my life at home, my days at Grandma's house were predictable. I knew I could count on certain things: big breakfasts in the morning, hugs every day, and church on Sunday. The front door was always open to family and friends and the pantry was stocked with good food for them to eat. A fresh pitcher of Grandma's special fruit tea was always in the refrigerator, along with one of two desserts, peach cobbler or lemon pound cake, and once a week a pot of homemade vegetable soup could be found simmering on the stove.

This predictability also included a set daily pattern created by Grandma that she and Aunt Macy affectionately referred to as their "routine." Each morning, without exception, the routine began with a good bowel movement. Grandma encouraged me to do the same, as she was convinced a person had to be "regular" to be healthy. So, the first thing every morning, I sat on the toilet and strained and strained, until my eyeballs bulged and the blood vessels swelled in my neck, with no results.

I wanted to be a part of the "routine" too, but it was impossible for me to have a movement every day, because I was accustomed to holding my bowels until Mama gave me permission to use the toilet. She always went to the bathroom with me too, so it was hard to produce anything while she was standing right there watching.

I told Grandma about my problem, and she helped me out by giving me a tablespoon of castor oil, chased with orange juice to mask the taste. After a few doses and a lot of patience, soon I was as regular as Monday morning.

I loved the routine, and everything else about my new life and I positively idolized my Grandma Storm. She wore dresses and pearls, even if she didn't have anywhere to go and she always found the time in the mornings to pin her hair into an elegant bun, or to sweep it up with two tortoiseshell combs. On Sundays, when she dressed for church, she put on lacy white gloves that buttoned at the wrist and brightly colored hats with mesh veils in the front; some of them had rhinestone pins or feathers. She always put on perfume when she went out too, favoring floral scents like jasmine or Lily of The Valley.

She wasn't pretty in a delicate way like Mama, but handsome, with chiseled cheekbones and deep-set eyes. She was tall for a woman born during her time, but she wasn't awkward in her height and she didn't slump like some tall people do. She carried herself with confident grace.

Wherever Grandma was, there was music. She hummed or whistled as she cooked and worked her garden and a song was always waiting at her piano ready for my request. She played strictly by ear, the music magically flowing from her fingertips.

Wherever she was, love presided. She was not one to openly display affection, except for a hug here and there, but her love had a gentle constancy I could feel. I knew it was there, as surely as I knew the crystal dish on her cocktail table in the living room was full of cream-filled chocolate drops and candied orange slices.

18

In July, I celebrated my ninth birthday. Like every other year, I had my favorite German chocolate cake, only this time Grandma Storm baked it instead of Mama.

After we finished our cake and ice cream, I followed Grandma outside to walk the grounds around her house and tend to her flowers. I liked to help her water them and pluck off the dead buds, stooping every now and then to pull a weed.

Almost as much as she loved her flowers, she loved the birds, all of them, from the loud, aggressive blue jay to the shy sparrow. She had brought a sack filled with crackers and bread crumbs that we scattered out on the lawn for them to eat. They filled the trees around the house, squawking loudly, waiting to be fed.

While we were pulling some weeds, we heard a weak chirping coming from the azalea bushes. Grandma got a stick and separated the limbs, probing for the source of the sound. Suddenly out fell a small grayish ball.

"It's a baby robin," she said.

What had fallen out of the bushes didn't look anything like a robin. It had pink, almost transparent skin, with blue veins showing through, and patches of gray fuzz on its head and randomly on its body. But I figured Grandma was right because she knew her birds.

"How did it get here?" I asked.

"Poor thing must have fallen from a tree," she said. She pointed overhead to a high branch. "See, there's the nest full of the rest of the baby robins."

"What should we do?"

"Let it be," she said. "I'm sure the mother will come looking for it when she realizes it's missing."

I didn't want to leave the baby bird alone, but I did because Grandma told me to. I sat on the front porch and watched, waiting for the mother to come and retrieve it.

After a few minutes, I saw the mother robin fly to the nest of baby birds that Grandma had pointed out. I knew it was her because she had a dull red breast and Grandma had told me the female robin was a duller color than the male. She was carrying a fat earthworm in her mouth to feed her babies. They gobbled it down and she flew away again. A few more minutes passed, and then the mother bird brought back another worm, dropping it into the open beaks of the babies.

I could hear the baby bird that had fallen from the nest chirping desperately from the ground, trying to get her attention, but she made no attempt to fly down and feed it.

Angry at the mother bird for her negligence, I barreled into the house to tell Grandma.

"Give her time," she said. "She'll come for the baby eventually."

"How will she get it back up to the nest?" I asked.

"Now, *that* I don't know, but I'm sure she'll find a way."

I went outside and sat on the porch again. A half hour passed. The baby's chirping got louder and more desperate, but still the mother bird didn't come for it or try to feed it. I went into the house once more to give Grandma a report.

"What if she knows the baby's gone, and she doesn't care?" I asked. "What if the mother pushed it out because she doesn't want it anymore?"

"That's nonsense. It's her baby, of course she wants it."

All of a sudden, we heard loud squawking coming from the backyard. Grandma ran outside to see what was going on and I was right on her heels. When we got out there, we discovered the baby bird had wandered into the middle of the yard and a blue jay was attacking it. While we stood there, two more birds swooped down and took a turn pecking at the baby.

"Grandma, they're killing it! We've got to do something!"

She took off her house slipper and fanned it in the air, chasing after the blue jays. "Shoo! Get out of here!" she hollered. I followed close behind her, waving my arms like a whirligig.

When the blue jays had all flown off, I picked up the baby bird and cradled it in my hands.

"You may as well keep it," said Grandma. "Your scent is on it. The mother bird won't come for it for sure now."

That was fine with me. It was what I had wanted all along. "I'll take good care of her, Grandma. I promise; you won't have to do a thing."

"Her? How do you know it's a girl?" she asked.

I looked down at the fragile creature in my hands, its scrawny, wrinkled neck, bulbous, half-closed eyes and open yellow beak. "I can just tell."

"What are you going to call her?"

I studied for a minute and then announced, "I'm going to name her Ladybug."

She laughed. "Why are you naming her that? She's a bird, not a bug."

"Just because."

Grandma found a shoebox to keep Ladybug in and I lined it with grass to make it feel more like a nest. I fed her tiny bits of bologna and pieces of bread soaked in milk. She was always crying out for food. No matter how much I fed her, she still opened her beak wide whenever I came around her, begging for more.

About a week after I found Ladybug, I went to feed her some leftover toast from breakfast and she wouldn't take the food. When I picked her up, her head flopped to one side.

I took her to Grandma. "What's wrong with her?" I asked.

Grandma examined Ladybug. "I think she's dead," she said. "I'm sorry honey, but baby birds don't make it long without their mothers."

I thought Ladybug was just sleeping. I nudged her with my finger again and again, trying to wake her up, but she wouldn't move. For the rest of the day, I held her and cried.

"Sweetheart," Grandma said, "it was just a bird. You didn't even have it long to get attached to it."

Late afternoon Grandma told me it was time to take Ladybug outside and bury her before she stunk up the house. I got a spoon from the kitchen drawer and dug a hole in the yard near the azalea bush where I first found her. After I had buried her, I made a tiny headstone with rocks and stuck dandelions in her grave. Grandma didn't understand; Ladybug was more than just a bird to me.

19

Before I knew it, summer was over and I was in the car with Daddy, heading back home to get ready for school.

When he drove up, I was glad to see him because I had missed him over the summer. But I was sad in a way too, because I didn't want to leave Grandma's house. And I was worried that I didn't have notebooks and pencils and whatever else was required for the fourth grade. Daddy promised me he had checked into it and bought all the necessary supplies and everything was ready for me at home. He tried to cheer me up by telling me he'd bought me three new dresses and a pair of shoes for school, and it worked. It gave me something to look forward to.

Mama and the boys were already in bed when we got home. It took me hours to fall asleep that night, knowing school was starting the next day. My mind raced with thoughts of what fourth grade would be like.

Mama woke me up in the morning. "Time to get ready for school," she said in a somewhat kind voice.

The minute I saw her I realized how much I'd missed her. Thinking maybe she had changed over the summer, I said, cheerfully, "Good morning, Mama," and ran to her. I tried to put my arms around her waist, but she pushed me back. Then she handed me one of the dresses Daddy had bought me, still in the cellophane wrapper, along with a pair of white knee socks. She told me to take off my dirty clothes and to give them to her. Without delay I obeyed her.

As soon as she left the room, I picked up my new dress, tore off the plastic wrapper and removed the pins, one at a time, putting them in a neat pile on my bed. Then I slid out the piece of cardboard that kept the dress crisp and square. It was a simple plaid, madras shift in pastel colors of pink and orange, with two low pockets in front, below the waist and a white rounded collar with a tiny, pink satin bow right in the center.

It was an ordinary school dress, but to me it was special, because I knew Daddy was thinking of me when he picked it out. As I slipped it over my head, careful not to wrinkle it, I imagined how all the other kids at school would admire and compliment me and how proud I would feel.

I sat on my bed to put on my knee socks. As I was folding down the tops of each one, Mama returned, carrying my new brown oxford shoes. They were shiny and stiff and smelled like leather. I loosened the laces and stepped my feet in, and when I bent down to tie them, it occurred to me something was missing.

"I don't have any panties on!" I blurted out to Mama. "You forgot to bring my panties!"

"Oh, my," she said in her sarcastic voice, a voice that always made me nervous. "Your daddy must have forgotten to buy you any new panties for school." She put her hand on her cheek— one of her favorite theatrical gestures—and said, "Oh, no!

What are we going to do? I threw all your old ones away! They were ratty!"

I glanced across the room to the corner, where I had left the paper bag of clothes I brought back from Grandma Storm's. It was gone. I looked at Mama, dumbfounded. Suddenly I was no longer excited about my new clothes or the fourth grade.

"I guess you'll have to go to school without panties today," Mama said. "Now hurry and get in the car. It's time to leave."

Mama took my older brother, Nick, who was now in junior high, to school first. Then she drove Jimmy D. and me to elementary school and dropped us off at the front door.

As I walked down the hall searching for my classroom, I could feel a draft between my legs. When I found the right room and entered, all the kids' eyes were on me. I was sure they could see through my dress. I hurried to find a seat in the last row and then sat, pressing my thighs together, tucking my dress snugly around them.

At recess, I wanted to join my classmates on the playground, but I looked down and saw the sun shining through the thin cotton of my new dress, outlining the curve of my hips, and in my mind, my bare vagina. Afraid someone would discover my secret I sat on a concrete step by the door of the school, and watched the other kids play.

The girls had on crisp new dresses, like mine, and they wore brightly colored ribbons in their hair that trailed behind them as they ran. They screamed out when a random brisk wind whipped and snapped their skirts, sometimes lifting them high enough to expose their panties. Carefree, and happy, they sailed down the slides and climbed on the monkey bars, played tag, and jumped rope; some of them were on the swings, pumping and stretching their legs out in front of them. I could hear them giggling and see their smiles when they talked to each other, but I couldn't make out what they were saying. Like my brothers, they were in a world far away from mine.

It took me a while to adjust back to my dismal life at home. Everything was the same as it had been before I left—face to the wall and everything—but it seemed much worse, because I had gotten a taste of what it was like to be a normal kid again. All I could think about that fall was my summer at Grandma Storm's.

Being exposed to other kids in school, and listening to them talk about their parents and their lives at home, reminded me of how happy I had been before Audrey died and before Mama's accident. It also made me realize how wrong my life had become. But still, I wasn't sure what I should do about it. I loved Mama, and I kept waiting, hoping, for her to get better and go back to the way she used to be.

Thanks to Grandma and Aunt Macy, by the end of the summer I was able to see a cute little girl whenever I looked in the mirror. But when I got home, Mama was quick to remind me I was ugly. To keep her from seeing my face, I found my mask in my room and started wearing it again. I put in on every day when I got in from school, this time, not because she told me to, but because I wanted to.

One afternoon, a friend of Nick's came over to the house for a visit and saw me wearing it. He asked Nick why his sister had a dish towel on her face.

Mama overheard the conversation and bailed him out. "We don't know why she does it. She put it on one day and has been wearing it ever since. I guess we're used to it." Then she lowered her voice to a whisper. "She's always doing strange stuff like that."

She turned to me. "Why *are* you wearing that thing over your face anyway?" she asked, as if she didn't have the slightest clue as to why I would do such a thing. "Take it off right now!"

"Yes, ma'am," I answered mechanically. But I didn't want to take off my mask. I stalled, pretending to fumble with the knot.

"Give it to me," she said, sticking out one of her hands, palm up. "Now!" she demanded, jutting her hand forward. I wasn't moving fast enough for her, so she jerked the mask down from my face herself. It dangled around my neck, held on by a double knot. "Now, take it the rest of the way off."

As soon as I got it untied, she snatched it from me and tossed it into the trash. One ragged edge hung over the side and clung there for a while before its own weight took it down, out of my sight.

I missed my mask immediately, the closeness, the warmth, the smell of it, and the sense of security it gave me. But most of all, I missed the barrier it put between Mama and me. Without it, I felt frightened and vulnerable, like a newborn suddenly stripped of the safe, familiar boundaries of a womb.

2O

My fourth grade was spent isolated from the other kids, most of the time with my dress collar pulled up over my face to simulate to the protected feeling my mask had given me.

The day after school was out, Daddy took me back to Grandma's and I remained there for the summer. He called on the phone once a week to talk to me and make sure I was doing okay. But I didn't speak to Mama at all during my entire stay.

Like before, Daddy didn't come for me until the night before school started. He told me in the car on the way home that I would be staying with Grandma Storm every summer until Mama got better.

"Why can't I live with Grandma and go to school in Nashville?" I asked Daddy.

"Grandma Storm hasn't been feeling well and she isn't able to take care of you by herself. And your aunt Macy has to work. Besides, I'm still hoping your mama will get better soon and everything will get back to normal."

The previous spring, Mama had announced to the family she was going to have another baby, her fifth, counting Audrey. By the time I got back home, she was almost seven months along.

She was depressed for the last few months of her pregnancy and went back to spending most of her days in bed. She had the baby, another son, that winter and named him Ryan, after one of her favorite actors, Ryan O'Neal.

The house was almost happy after Ryan was born. You could feel the presence of a new life and hope for change was in the air. When Daddy was at work, Mama had to take care of the baby all by herself, and I was glad because it distracted her for a while. She kept busy fixing his bottles and doing laundry and other chores, but wherever she was, she made sure I was within her sight.

Daddy beamed with pride over Ryan, as he did with all his kids. He kept saying he was glad he was born a boy. He said he had always dreamed of having enough sons to make up a basketball team. It made me think I had been a disappointment to him because I was a girl.

In the mornings he became preoccupied with feeding and caring for Ryan and quit coming to my room to give me a kiss. Still, I woke up early every day, listening and waiting, hoping it would be the morning he would decide to come see me again. In the evenings he often worked late and Mama usually sent me to bed before he got home, so it got to where I hardly saw him at all.

Sometimes at night I cried because I missed Daddy so much, missed being held by him and hearing the loving words he had once said to me. I cried because I missed Grandma too. I longed for her orderliness, the smell of the flowers in her garden and the comfort of her food. I cried because I didn't know what to do to make Mama love me the way she loved Audrey and my brothers, the way she had loved me before.

Like everybody else in the family, I was positively fascinated with my new baby brother, but Mama kept me far away from him, like she did with Nick and Jimmy D. The more she kept me away, the more fixated on being near him I became. All I wanted was to hold him and cuddle him and kiss his soft head.

While I was sweeping the house one day, I saw my opportunity to find out what it was like to touch him. He was in my parents' room, asleep on their bed. Mama was in the kitchen, at the other end of the house, talking on the phone. After I made sure she was in deep conversation, I propped the broom against the wall and tiptoed to Ryan.

He was even cuter up close. He had full pink cheeks and a tiny, beak-like mouth. The sight of him sleeping—pillows piled all around him like fluffy clouds—reminded me of a picture I'd seen in Grandma's Bible of an angel in heaven.

Carefully I put my hand on his back and held it there, soaking up the warmth of his body. Then I bent over and touched my lips to the top of his head, inhaling his sweet, powdery scent. Being near him made me aware of his fragility, his innocence, of how entirely helpless he was, how he was at the mercy of those around him, now at the mercy of me.

All of a sudden, anger rose from my chest and then a disturbing vision popped into my head. I saw myself picking Ryan up and throwing him across the room. It was so real, this vision, I could feel the weight of him in my hand, see him sliding down the wall. The impulse to follow through with what I had imagined overwhelmed me. Before I knew what was happening, I had clutched his nightgown to lift him from the bed.

Then I stopped. *No! I can't hurt Ryan!* I let go of him and ran from the room, taking the erupting anger with me.

Standing in the hall, I felt as though I could burst. I needed somewhere to direct all the fury I held inside. So I turned it on myself. I doubled my fists and hit both sides of my head at once, banging until I could hear ringing in my ears. Next I pulled at my hair, my lips, and my eyelashes. Working my way down my body, I beat myself in the stomach and on the fronts of my thighs. I turned my ankles over, again and again, twisting them till the bones crunched.

Feeling much better, I picked up the broom and resumed sweeping the floor. I was ashamed of what I'd thought of doing, and wondered why something so sick had even entered my mind. Why, when I had nothing but adoration for my baby brother I had suddenly wanted to hurt him. And then, like a sledgehammer to the head, it struck me: *Maybe I am an evil killer after all.*

2**1**

With so much of Mama's attention going to Ryan, Daddy had to take on more of the responsibility of caring for the rest of the family. In addition to working his regular job, he got my brothers and me off to school in the mornings and made sure we were fed supper in the evenings. Whenever he had ball practice, or if he had to coach a game, he brought cafeteria food home from the school where he taught.

One afternoon I heard my brothers cheering when Daddy walked in the door from work with cafeteria food. Even though I knew I was going to get something good to eat, I was sad, because I also knew it meant Daddy would be leaving and would most likely be gone for the rest of the night.

After he had given the boys their meals, he walked over to where I was standing to give me mine. When he peeled away the tin foil covering the food, I was thrilled to see it was piled high with slices of roast beef and a generous serving of mashed potatoes smothered with brown gravy. As he handed me the steamy plate, along with a small carton of milk, he grinned and winked.

He still showed me signs of his affection: a rub on the head while Mama was asleep, a wink when she looked away.

Although I was well aware he was trying to conceal how he felt about me from her, I never got angry with him, or thought about why he didn't want her to know. I was too desperate for his love to care, and in a way the hiding made his gestures more special—our own shared secret.

I yearned for his attention and welcomed it, but at the same time, I knew how much it irritated Mama and that if she found out I would be the one who would end up paying for it later. I looked over at her to see if she had seen him wink at me. She had.

"Don't give her anything to drink until she has completely cleaned her plate," she said to Daddy.

A quizzical expression crossed his face, but without saying a word, he took the carton of milk from me and put it up on the chest of drawers in Mama's bedroom, then left for his ballgame.

After I had finished eating my food, I remembered the milk he had put aside for me, but I was too afraid to ask Mama if I could have it. As the night went on, I came to realize she had no intention of giving it to me at all.

About two weeks later, I was standing in my usual place in the hallway when Mama approached me from behind. I felt her shove something into my shoulder. "I found this in my room," she said. "I believe it belongs to you."

When I turned around, I saw she was holding a carton of milk. "Be sure and drink it all," she said. "Daddy brought it for you and you wouldn't want to hurt his feelings now, would you?"

I took it from her, although I thought she was joking, that she couldn't possibly be serious.

"Drink up," she said, waving her hand briskly.

I opened the carton, and a putrid odor sprang from it. I peered down through the spout, and saw the milk had curdled and begun to separate.

"I can't drink this," I said. "It's spoiled!"

"Drink it!" she shouted.

I took in a deep breath and held it. Slowly I lifted the carton to my mouth. But the smell of the spoiled milk was awful, and I could not bring myself to drink it. I closed the carton and dropped it to the floor in front of me. "No! I won't do it!"

She picked it up. "Drink it or I'll pour it down your throat myself."

She wasn't bluffing and I knew it. Since her accident, it seemed like she had lost the inner voice that prevents most people from committing mean acts. As if she had no rationalization period between thinking she was going to do something horrendous and actually doing it. In my mind's eye, I saw myself throwing the carton at her, and then her shocked expression with chunks of clabbered milk clinging to it. But unlike Mama, I could hear the voice inside my head, loud and clear, telling me not to do it.

From similar past experiences, I had learned, either I was going to have to drink the spoiled milk on my own, or do it her way and get a beating in the process. With tears streaming down my cheeks, I took it from her and forced it down, swallowing as fast as I could, first the bitter liquid, and then the congealed lumps.

When I had finished, she took the carton from me, checked to make sure it was empty and then grabbed one of my arms and spun me back around facing the wall again.

A few days later, Mama brought me milk again, this time in a glass. When I took it from her, our fingers touched, and for a second, our eyes met. The thought crossed my mind that it could be her way of apologizing for forcing me to drink the spoiled milk days earlier. I searched out her empty glare for a trace of kindness, and found none.

The glass felt cold in my hand. I brought it up to my nose and took a sniff. The milk didn't smell sour. Still I sipped warily. It tasted sweet and mellow and it was creamy gliding down my throat. I turned up the glass and guzzled, my heart soaring with joy, because it was the first time since before her accident Mama had done something nice for me.

Then just as I got to the bottom of the glass of milk, I felt a slimy lump slither through my lips and slide across my tongue, where it burst, releasing a rich, salty taste. Gagging, I pulled the milk away from my mouth. A clear string of slime ran down my chin.

"I read that raw eggs are good for you," she said. "They make your hair shiny."

22

To better support his growing family, Daddy took an office job as personnel manager for a local aluminum plant. Although he made more money and his new employment was less demanding of his time, it put an end to the cafeteria food he had been bringing home for the family to eat.

Mama resumed preparing the family's meals. Now that she was in complete control of what I ate, I rarely got what the rest of the family had. Instead I was given the uneaten scraps from everyone else's plates—fat, gristle and half-chewed meat. She also continued to plant strange things in my food and drink. She brought me sweet tea with bacon grease in it, a bowl of soup filled with hot peppers and mashed potatoes with scoops of lard mixed in.

Then she began withholding food. Soon it was routine for me to be sent to bed without supper. On those nights, hunger ripped at my insides, as I lay unable to sleep, and my thoughts were dominated by trying to come up with ways to get more to eat.

When I cleaned the house, I sometimes came across edible morsels on the floor, like soggy pieces of cereal my brothers had dropped from their breakfast bowls. When Mama wasn't paying attention, I scavenged around in the trash cans for discarded sandwich crusts and apple cores.

My best opportunity to get anything of significant substance was right after everyone else in the family had finished supper, when Mama had me take the leftover scraps outdoors to feed our dog, Rusty. However, under her watchful eyes, swiping the dog's food was no easy feat. She had calculated how long it took me to walk to the end of the backyard to dump the scraps, and if I didn't finish within the allotted time she came out to check.

Sometimes there were no leftovers from supper, no crumbs on the floor, or opportunities to dig through the trash, and so I went to bed hungry. One night, after many of listening to my stomach growl, it occurred to me that the kitchen, right beside my room, was full of food. I decided to take the risk and slip in there to find something decent to eat.

Well past midnight, I tiptoed down the hall and peeked into Mama and Daddy's bedroom to make sure they were sound asleep. On the way back, I passed my brothers in their bunk beds; I could hear their deep and even breathing. Gathering all my courage, I made my way to the kitchen, careful not to bump into anything that might create a sound and awaken someone. Just inside the doorway, I stubbed my toe on Jimmy D.'s schoolbook satchel, slumped in the floor where he'd left it earlier. I froze in fear and listened for the sound of Mama's bed squeaking. The house remained silent so I continued with my mission.

As soon as I came to the refrigerator, I opened it and using my bare hands, dipped into hamburger goulash and mashed potatoes left over from supper, and crammed them into my mouth as fast as I could. After I had eaten all that my belly could hold, I scrambled back into bed, proud of my accomplishment and fell to sleep satisfied.

My secret visits to the kitchen became more frequent, as Mama fed me less and less. Eventually I was slipping out of my bed for food almost every night. Each time I got a little braver, staying in the kitchen longer, eating all the leftovers Mama had planned to heat up for lunch the next day. Soon she noticed the food was missing and became suspicious.

When she caught me, I was standing in front of the open refrigerator with my mouth full of pecan pie. Her face, illuminated by the refrigerator light, suddenly appeared. "Spit it out!" she said, shoving a trashcan under my mouth with one hand and squeezing my jaw until my cheeks collapsed with the other.

I expelled the gooey pie and it plunked against the bottom of the trashcan.

"You're like a sneaky weasel, stealing our food while we sleep. You're even beginning to look like a weasel," she said. She smacked me on the back of my head with the flat of her hand. "Pop goes the weasel."

23

Around lunchtime, on a Saturday, Mama brought me a plate, and on it was a huge slab of the hog jowl she used to season beans and turnip greens. "Eat it," she ordered.

Even though I was starving, the mere sight of the hog jowl with its dense, yellow fat, encased in thick, bristly skin, repulsed me. But when she went and got the flyswatter, and stood over me with the wire end poised in the strike position, I knew I had no choice but to eat it.

In an attempt to swallow it whole and avoid the taste and texture of the fat, I stabbed it with my fork and put the entire piece into my mouth. But the bulk of it got stuck in my throat and my body rejected it, and it plopped back onto the plate. I then tried to cut it into bite-size parts, but it was too tough, so I removed and ate the rubbery outer layer of skin, only to have it come back up too, the bristles scraping my throat along the way.

After half an hour of chewing and throwing up, and more chewing and more throwing up—Mama standing over me the entire time—I was able to get the hog jowl down.

For supper the same day, she brought me another plate of food. This time it was the good stuff: fried chicken, mashed potatoes, pinto beans and cornbread.

I wanted to dig right in, but I knew better. After so many episodes of either being forced to eat something gross, or finding strange things planted in my food and drink, I was left to face the hurtful truth: even a seemingly kind act from Mama most likely had a covert cruel intention.

As I ate, I prodded around with my fork. The food seemed fine, but I noticed she was watching my every move, which made me suspect something was up.

When I had the last bite of mashed potatoes in my mouth, I felt a hard object scrape against my teeth. With my tongue, I rolled it around, trying to figure out what it was. It was about half an inch long and ovular and it tasted metallic. The object was small enough to swallow, but something told me not to, so I slipped it under my tongue and continued eating until I had finished all my food, and then put down my fork.

Puzzled, Mama took the empty plate from me. She lifted and checked under the fork, and then darted her eyes back to me. "Where is the bullet?"

It's a bullet! "What bullet?" I asked, innocently.

"Open your mouth," she demanded. "Lift your tongue."

As I lifted my tongue, I allowed the bullet to slide out, and then nestled it between my teeth and jaw. Somehow, she missed it.

"You ate a bullet, you stupid bitch, you stupid, *stupid* bitch!"

I'm the stupid one? You've got nothing better to do with your time than to feed your kid a bullet in some mashed potatoes and I'm stupid?

As if she had heard what I was thinking, she slapped me solid across the face. Then she turned and walked away, disappearing into the kitchen.

I could hear her opening and shutting cabinet doors, shuffling cooking utensils around in the drawers, and then the rhythmic ping, ping, ping of a spoon hitting against a glass. It sounded like she was mixing something.

When she emerged from the kitchen, she was carrying a jelly jar filled to the brim with a mustard-color concoction. With her free hand, she grabbed the hair at the base of my head and led me through the kitchen and down to the basement.

When we got to the bottom of the stairs, she pushed the jelly jar into my face. "Drink this," she said.

Afraid to do otherwise, I took the mixture from her and drank. I expected it to taste much worse than it did, but it was pleasant, compared to some of the other stuff she'd forced on me. It was made of mustard, with hot sauce, and maybe some vinegar. Whatever it was, it must have been something meant to induce vomiting, because I lost my supper halfway through the glass. While I was throwing up, I managed to keep the bullet under my tongue.

When my stomach was empty, Mama went to the kitchen and got a butter knife. She then stooped down in front of me and used the knife to prod around in the slimy bits of chicken and beans and cornbread I had thrown up. In a twisted way, I enjoyed those few moments she was at my feet on her knees, poking around in my vomit.

She poked and poked, so intent on finding the bullet, I was fearful that if she didn't come across it soon, she might split my gut open. I decided to release it from my mouth, as if I had just thrown it up. As soon as the bullet hit the concrete, she snatched it up like it was a precious jewel. Then she took the remaining mustard mixture from me and without saying a word, stiff-armed me across my jaw.

I lost my balance and stumbled to one side. She got behind me and pushed me forward into the vomit. The palms of my hands and my knees smacked against the concrete floor.

"You dumb weasel!" she screamed.

She bent over, and with one of her hands, applied pressure to the back of my head, trying to force my face into the vomit. As she pushed me down, I locked my elbows and resisted her with all my strength. She pressed harder, using her weight. As she shoved, my arms bowed and I moved closer and closer to the vomit, until the tip of my nose was touching it. Finally, I couldn't hold her back any longer and collapsed. My forehead slammed against the concrete floor into the slimy mess.

With my face in the vomit, I kept fighting, until I managed to slip loose and raise my head again. She grabbed a broom leaning up against the wall and pointed the handle toward me. I had been hit with the handle of a broom before, plenty of times; I remembered how the thin wood sliced into my skin. But I wasn't ready to give up yet. Down on all fours, I stared at her square in the eyes, like a wild animal ready to attack, vomit dripping from my chin.

She hit me across the back.

I grunted from the pain.

She raised the broom up over her head and hit me a second time, and then a third, and a fourth. And just when I thought I couldn't take another blow, she gave up.

She went up to the kitchen and got a roll of paper towels. "Clean up this mess!" she said, tossing it down the stairs to me.

I had vomit on my face and I had just taken a helluva beating, but I still felt like a winner, because for the first time ever, I had been in control of Mama. The brief gratification I got from watching her down on her knees sifting through my vomit gave me a sensation of power I'd never before experienced, and made me realize how strong I had become and that I was capable of much more than I'd known.

24

No one at school paid much attention to all the bruises up and down my legs and arms. Lots of kids had cuts and bruises from falling down and bumping into things. Mama was careful to whip me with the flyswatter or a wire hanger only where my clothes would hide the marks. When occasionally she lost control and busted my lip, or blacked one of my eyes, she kept me home from school until the wounds had healed.

During the school months, her physical attacks were the least of my problems. She had become more creative in her efforts to humiliate me in front of my classmates. She started out the year by making me wear the same dress to school every day. This went on for weeks. When that got old, she chopped my hair into all different lengths, so short in places it stuck straight up like the bristles of a porcupine. Whenever Daddy and my brothers asked her about it, she told them I had cut it myself.

Her manipulation of my appearance ensured that I was a total outcast among my peers. I often heard them whisper— hands cupped around their mouths—as they passed by me in the halls, "There's the 'weirdo girl.'"

I did my best to fade into the background. I alienated myself from the other kids and didn't speak to anyone unless it was absolutely necessary. The girls in my class formed cliques and talked about their favorite TV shows and the slumber parties they went to. I had nothing to share, so I thought it was best to keep my mouth shut; that way no one would find out how different I really was.

In a sense I didn't mind so much being an outcast at school. It saved me the trouble of having to explain to the other kids why I couldn't talk on the phone or invite them over to my house, or tell them why my hair was stubby and my clothes were odd. Friends would have only made my life more complicated than it already was.

Still, in spite of all the humiliation and the loneliness, being in school was much better than being at home. It was nice to sit down in chairs like other people, and to be able to go to the bathroom, or get a drink of water whenever I needed to. I was fascinated with the water fountains at school; ice cold water was a luxury I never got at home. Each time I passed a fountain in the halls, I could not control the impulse to stop and drink until my stomach felt cold and hard like a watermelon.

My favorite part of school was eating in the cafeteria. Food was the only thing that brought me pleasure. But eating lunch at school was not enough, because Mama continued to withhold my suppers and I was always hungry. Grandma had fattened me up during my summer stay with her, but within months I had lost all the weight I'd gained while I was there and had already started to look gaunt. My face was drawn and forlorn. My skin was sallow, my hair was stringy and dull and I had bald spots from having it pulled out so much.

About halfway through the school year, Mama decided to start making me late for class every day, so however ridiculous my appearance, it would surely be noticed when I walked in ten minutes after the bell had rung.

Ms. Wicks was my fifth grade teacher. I admired her because she was young and pretty. She had brown, wavy hair and the skin on her face was always pink and shiny, like she had just scrubbed it. She wore soft, fuzzy sweaters of pastel blue and lavender, some of them with embroidered rosebuds and tiny rhinestones.

At the beginning of the year, Ms. Wicks liked me too. But after a while, the constant tardiness began to annoy her. She thought it was an intentional act of disrespect on my part. First she disciplined me by taking away my recess. Then, when that didn't work, she called Mama.

The next day, after she had talked to Mama on the phone, she stayed in at recess with me, after everyone else had gone outside. "Tuesday, this tardiness every morning is going to have to stop," she said. "It disrupts my class when you walk in late."

"I'm sorry, Ms. Wicks, I can't help it."

"Yes you *can* help it, Tuesday. I know you can because I spoke with your mother on the phone last night and she told me you walk to school every morning. Isn't that right? Don't you walk to school?"

I squirmed in my seat, like it suddenly had become a hot griddle. "Yes, ma'am."

She got up from her desk and walked around in front, leaning back against it. "Mrs. Storm said she has you dressed and out of the house in the mornings early enough for you to be able to get to school by eight o'clock."

I fiddled with the corners of some papers on my desk. "But I don't have enough time," I pleaded.

"I know better! I also checked with your brothers' teachers and found out they are hardly ever late. If they can make it on time, then surely you can."

I tried to tell her the reason my brothers weren't late was because they rode the bus to school, but when I opened my mouth to speak she cut me off. "No more excuses! I've given you plenty of opportunities to correct this and all you've given me is excuses!" She stood straight and calmed her voice to a controlled, serious tone. "You will continue to stay in at recess, and in addition, you will write an essay on why it's important not to be late for school. You'll do this every day until you learn to make it on time."

The next morning, as usual, Mama didn't let me leave our house in time to get to school by eight o'clock. I ran as fast as I could and I was close, but I didn't make it to class before the bell rang. The following morning, I tried even harder and again I failed. After weeks and weeks of punishment, I guess Ms. Wicks felt guilty, because she gave in and allowed me to have my recess back. She learned to work around my tardiness, but she held it against me for the remainder of the year.

All the frustrations with being late to school and then becoming a spectacle because of my appearance when I got there, spurred horrifying nightmares. I had the same one over and over practically every night. I called it my black pit dream:

It's the first day of school and I cannot find my classroom. I am late. I am driven by the urgent need to push forward, to beat the clock. The school seems large, the corridors vast. They widen before my eyes and the lockers soar endlessly upward. The fluorescent lights are as far away as the sky. I'm late. I search for the office to ask for help, but I can't find it either. Feeling the pressure of time running out, I try to hurry…faster…faster, but I can only move in slow motion. Finally I spot the office. It's huge; the doorknob takes two hands to turn. I open my mouth to speak to the lady behind the desk, but the words that come out make no sense, as if I am speaking another language. Frustrated, I turn and run. I see a stairway; I go up. As I climb the steps, they cave in under me. I trip and tumble down them, landing in front of a room I believe to be my class. When I walk in, all the kids laugh, laugh loudly. "Wrong class," they shout at once. They point at my clothes, my choppy hair, and they keep on laughing. I run from the room and continue to search for what seems like days, until the bell rings. School is out. The other students pour out of the classrooms. They knock me down. I can feel them trampling on my body like I am rubble. I manage to get on my feet again and join the other kids. Pushing through the double doors, I follow them outside. All of a sudden, the earth opens up in front of me and below is a black pit. I fall, spinning in somersaults gobbled up into the black hole.

One night, after waking from the nightmare in a cold sweat, I remembered God and what Grandma Storm had told me about Him always being there for me. As she had taught me, I made sure to thank Him for all his bounty first.

"Oh Heavenly Father," I began, like I'd learned in church. "Thank you for school, and for the cafeteria and a warm place to sleep. God bless Daddy, and Mama, Jimmy D., Nick, and my new baby brother, Ryan. Bless Grandma Storm and Aunt Macy. Please take care of my sister, Audrey and Ladybug, who are up in heaven with you now. Lord, I know I did something bad when I wished Audrey would die, and when I gave her the flu. But I wasn't sure I was sick when I let her chew that piece of bubble-gum and I sure didn't think she would die. Anyway, I'm sorry about it, Lord. Please forgive me." Then I got to what needed. "God, can you please, please make Mama stop hurting me and make her love me again? Amen."

Every night for a month, I said the prayer, but nothing changed. I thought maybe God hadn't heard me, even though Grandma Storm had assured me no prayer went unheard. So just in case, I prayed louder and waited. But every day when I got up, my life was still the same.

Grandma Storm had explained to me how God works in ways sometimes we humans don't understand. She said there's a reason for everything that happens and not to doubt Him, but to be patient and He would someday show me the reason. I wanted to believe her. I wanted to believe God had a purpose for allowing my life to be so miserable. But I couldn't imagine what the purpose could be. I came to the conclusion that God was angry with me for what I had done to Audrey, and that's why He didn't answer my prayer.

25

I was in the car with Daddy, on my way to Grandma Storm's house for my regular summer visit, when he told me she had been sick the past few months. He said she had something called polyps of the colon and had just learned the polyps had turned into cancer. She had recently begun to go down fast. He said I was going to have to help Aunt Macy out around the house more and I should try not to be too much of a bother.

Our conversation did not prepare me for what awaited me at Grandma's house. When I arrived, she did not rush to greet me with open arms, like she had every other time before. I found her in the den, slumped over on the sofa, gazing at the television set. She didn't even look up when I walked into the room. She was wearing a blue floral house robe I'd seen her wear many times before. She had once filled it with her fleshy figure, but now it hung loosely from her sharp spine and protruding shoulder blades, like a shirt thrown over a bedpost. Without color on them, her lips faded into her face and her sparse hair was pinned into a scraggly bun on top of her head.

Grandma's vibrant spirit that had once filled her house with music and laughter had all but vanished. She didn't have the energy to get up early and prepare her colossal breakfasts anymore. She no longer whistled or sang as she puttered about the house and her piano was gathering dust.

Her flowers had been almost completely taken over by weeds. Some of the small ones had wilted and shriveled under the heat, and the taller ones bowed their heads low as if they no longer had a reason to reach for the sky. Aunt Macy and I took turns watering the garden, but it didn't do much good.

Even the birds were of no concern to Grandma anymore. They still waited every morning for her to come out and feed them like she had for so many years. They gathered in the yard, covering the grass like a dark, fluttering sheet, filling the air with their loud, angry chirping. Aunt Macy and I shooed them away, but they only came back as soon as we went inside the house.

While I was there, Grandma spent most of her days sleeping or sitting in silence. When she didn't have the strength to get up out of bed herself, Aunt Macy and I carried her into the den, where she sat on the sofa and watched her favorite soap operas. When she was too weak to hold herself up, we propped her with pillows. There she would sit for hours, without uttering a word, her eyes set deep in hollow sockets and fixed on the television, and her slack, gray skin sagging from the bones of her face.

It was a cheerless summer with Grandma Storm sick, but I was still thankful that I was able to stay with her and Aunt Macy. Even at their worst, being with them was much better than being at home. As always, the summer passed too quickly and before I knew it, Daddy was there to take me back to Spring Hill for school.

26

The bad news came early one morning in May, right before I left for school.

"That was Macy," Daddy said, after he put down the phone. "It's Mom. She's gone." His voice cracked when he added, "She went peacefully in her sleep."

When I heard about Grandma, I should have been crushed, because I loved her more than anyone else. But I wasn't. To me, she had already died the previous summer. The instant I saw her slumped over on the sofa, I knew her spirit had abandoned her broken-down old body and all that remained was an empty shell. I recognized the look and smell of death from those final days I had spent with Audrey. Over the course of the summer, the sadness from losing Grandma Storm had gradually oozed out. Now all I felt was anger. I was angry because she had left me, angry because I would never see her again, and because I now had to spend my summers at home in the hallway outside Mama's bedroom staring at a blank wall.

Since Mama's accident, Nick and Jimmy D. seldom wandered far from her side. During the cold months, after school, sometimes they joined her in her bed to watch television, nudging each other out of the way like puppies at feeding time, fighting for the space closest to her. Now that the weather was warm, they played outdoors, but only in spurts, coming in to touch base with her regularly.

One afternoon, I was standing in my usual place in the hall when I heard her ask them, "Which one of you loves your mama the most?"

"Me, me, I do!" they both said at once.

"Well, let's see about that. I'm having a contest," she announced. "I want each of you to take turns hitting Weasel in the stomach, and I will be the judge of who hits the hardest. Whoever hits the hardest loves me most."

Nick and Jimmy D. were five years apart in age, but close enough to be rivals. Most of their competitions were over who was the toughest or the most athletically inclined. They traded frog punches until their arm muscles were quivering and flicked each other's knuckles until they were blood red. The mention of any test of their skills excited them, and so did the chance to earn Mama's approval.

"Cool!" they both said.

Mama had me turn around and face my brothers, who were now in the hallway in front of me, ready to play "the game." They both looked nervous, but I could tell they were trying to hide it from each other.

Nick, around thirteen at the time, volunteered to go first. Without hesitation, he balled up his fist and hit me full strength in the stomach. I moaned from the pain. He immediately turned to Mama, grinning with pride in the force of his punch. She nodded to show her approval.

Jimmy D., who was much more tender-hearted by nature than Nick, was up next. I could tell from the expression on his face that he didn't want to do it. But he didn't want to look like a wimp in front of Nick and he wanted to please Mama and be the winner of "the game." He cocked back his arm and fired his punch, letting up right when he made contact with my stomach.

I tried to help him out by faking excruciating pain, but Mama wasn't fooled for a minute.

She scowled at him. "I'll give you another chance," she said. "Best two out of three."

The second time Nick again hit me as hard as he could. Jimmy D. put only slightly more behind his punch than he had before.

After the third round, Mama became aggravated with Jimmy D.'s weak punches and jumped up from bed. "You can't hit any harder than that?" she said. "You sissy! Here, let me show you how it is done." She came at me with a roundhouse that took me down to the floor. Then she declared Nick the winner and sent Jimmy D. to his room for the rest of the day.

Later on that night, I lay awake wondering what my brothers thought of Mama's treatment of me, or if they even thought of me at all. I never got to talk to them about it to find out, but Mama had once told me they didn't want to be around me because I was always dirty and reeked of urine.

It was true, I did stink. I wet the bed almost every night. But it wasn't entirely my fault. Mama didn't allow me to go to the bathroom without her permission, and there were days when she forgot to let me go at all, not even before she sent me to bed, so an accident was inevitable.

The mornings after an accident, Mama made me take my mattress outside to air. Sometimes the backyard was full of the neighborhood boys playing basketball with my brothers. It was then, when I passed by them, wrestling with the cumbersome pee-stained mattress, that I saw the obvious shame on my brothers' faces.

From holding my urine so much, I developed a problem with chronic kidney infections. At times they were so severe I ran a high fever. Once my temperature spiked all the way up to 104 degrees, and I slipped into a state of delirium.

Daddy called the family doctor, who said to give me aspirin and put cold washcloths on my forehead and chest. But in spite of Daddy's efforts, he couldn't bring my temperature back down to normal.

He took me to see the doctor and found out the infections were caused from not taking in enough liquids. The doctor said I needed to drink at least eight to ten glasses of water a day to flush out my system and warned that if I didn't, there might be permanent damage to my kidneys. He also told Daddy if I ever ran a high fever again not to let it go on for long, but to put me in a tub full of ice water to get my body temperature down.

When we got back home, Daddy relayed to Mama what the doctor had said, and she, in turn, promised him she would make sure I drank plenty of water.

That afternoon, she filled a large jar with tap water and gave it to me to drink. When I had finished it, she gave me another. She filled the jar again and again.

In a matter of minutes, I had to pee, but when I asked if I could go to the bathroom, she said no and gave me more water. "Drink up," she said, "doctor's orders."

As I struggled to hold my pee, sharp pains shot through my stomach and across my back. My clothing was drenched with sweat. I clamped my thighs together in a last desperate effort to keep from wetting on myself. But it was too late. I felt a warm stream running down my legs.

"For God's sake, go to the bathroom, Weasel, before you piss all over the place!" she shouted.

For about two weeks, she continued to force water down me, while making me retain my urine. Then she went back to depriving me of water, until I developed another bad kidney infection. Before long, I was running a high fever again, and Daddy had me sitting in a tub of ice water.

27

On July, 11, I woke up early, hopeful that Mama would be nicer to me since it was my birthday.

She came to my room and got me up like she did every morning. I had wet the bed the night before, so she told me to take my mattress outside to air.

When I came back inside, she ordered me to strip off my clothes and stand in the hall until she called for me. Then she went into the bathroom.

I could hear her filling the tub with water. It had been a while since I'd had a bath, and I was glad I was going to get clean, remembering what she had said about my brothers not wanting to be around me because of my odor.

"Get your filthy ass in here!" she yelled out to me.

As I walked toward the bathroom, I noticed an unusual amount of steam drifting down the hallway. A feeling of dread came over me. Something was not right.

The air in the bathroom was hot and heavy. It was hard to breathe. Mama was sitting on the edge of the tub. Ryan was standing close beside her with his body pressed firmly against hers.

She shut off the water. "Take your eyes off my son and get in the bathtub!"

My skin had become glazed with perspiration and despite the heat, I was shivering. I looked at the tub. Steam clouds were hovering above the water.

Mama poked me in the arm with her finger. "I said get in!"

"It's too hot!" I begged, "Please don't make me!"

She shoved me toward the tub.

I screamed. Startled, Ryan jumped and ran from the room.

"Don't make me throw you in!" she warned.

Slowly I lifted one leg over the side of the bathtub and then lowered it into the water, allowing my foot to barely touch the surface. The heat nipped at the tip of my toe and I jerked my foot out, hobbling backward.

Before I fully regained my balance, she grabbed me by my hair and hurled me into the tub, face first. The scalding water stung my skin like a million angry bees. I could feel her clutch tighten at the back of my neck as she smashed my face into the rubber mat at the bottom of the tub.

All at once, the threat of drowning closed in and I could no longer feel the heat from the water. Summonsing all my strength, I fought back, clawing at the wet porcelain all around me. Finally I slithered free from her grip. Holding on to the side of the tub, I pulled myself up, and sucked in air.

"What is wrong with you," she asked, trying to make her voice sound kind. "You need a bath, you smell like pee!" she said, and pushed me in again.

I scratched her face and arms and grabbed her blouse, pulling her down with me.

"Why are you fighting me?" she asked. "I'm just trying to wash your hair!"

But I knew better. I knew what she was doing to me wasn't right. Although my strength was no match for hers, my endurance was. I continued fighting, breaking free of her grip again and again, until she gave up and told me to get out and put my clothes back on.

Later, I was standing in the hallway, weak from fatigue, when I started swaying from side to side. Suddenly I collapsed to the floor.

Mama became enraged when she saw me. "What's the matter? Are you tired?" she said, in the same sarcastic way she had earlier in the day when she was trying to force my head into scalding water. "I'll show you what it really feels like to be tired." She sat up in bed and propped her pillow behind her back so she could better see me. "Get up and start doing deep knee bends," she said. "Do them until I tell you to stop. And I want you to squat low when you go down. I want to see your butt touch the backs of your heels."

As I exercised, something Grandma Storm had once told me came to my mind. "You're an awfully skinny girl, Tuesday," she had said, "but you have long, strong legs. It's the sign of a thoroughbred, you know."

I shut my eyes and tried to recreate her image from memory—her kind face that always glowed under the halo of her silver hair, the softness in her pewter eyes. "Long strong legs, long strong legs, long strong legs," I chanted under my breath.

After I had done nearly one hundred deep knee bends, my thighs and calves cramped. Another fifty and they went numb. Then when I was in the butt-to-heel position, my knees locked up, and once again, I fell to the floor in a beaten heap.

"Please, Mama, please let me stop," I begged. "I won't do it anymore, I promise." Just as soon as the words had escaped my lips, I wanted to eat them back up again. I knew I wasn't supposed to talk unless I was asked a question, but I couldn't help it; I was drunk from fatigue.

"How dare you talk to me?" she said, gnarling her face. "I didn't give you permission to speak."

There was nothing left to do now but await my punishment. I slumped against the wall, pulled my knees up close to my chest, buried my face in my arms and cried.

"Just go to bed, Weasel!" she screamed. "Get out of my sight!"

I jumped up and ran to my room. For the first time in my life, I was glad my birthday was over.

28

Mama tossed aside the magazine she'd been reading and sprang from her bed. Standing in my usual place outside her room, I watched out the corner of my eye as she went over to her chest of drawers and began rummaging through her clothes.

When she had found what she was searching for, she slung it to me. It slid across the hallway floor and wrapped around my ankles. "Put that on," she said.

It was a turquoise green two-piece swimsuit, an old one of hers. I picked it up and examined it, puzzled. I had no idea why she wanted me to put it on, but it didn't make any difference, because I always obeyed her commands, without questions, regardless of how outlandish her order seemed.

After I had changed into the suit, she went to the linen closet in the hallway and did some more rummaging. This time she pulled out an old blanket. Now I was even more confused.

"I'm sick of looking at you standing there in the hallway all of the time." She handed me the blanket. "Take this out into the backyard, spread it on the ground and lay in the sun." Then, as an afterthought she added, "Some color on your homely face couldn't hurt it."

"Yes, ma'am," I said, and then hurried along before she changed her mind.

I walked outside and the screen door snapped shut behind me. Suddenly I became frightened; the yard was much bigger than I had remembered.

I stood there on the patio for a minute. I looked over at Nick and Jimmy D., who were in a far corner of the yard, under the mimosa tree where Daddy had built the tree house, talking to some neighborhood boys. They all turned at once when they heard the screen door slam. When they saw it was me who had come out, their faces immediately took on expressions of bewilderment.

I went out into the yard to the same spot where, on my eighth birthday, I had sat tying together dandelions to make a necklace. It had been only three years since then, but it felt like a lifetime ago. So much had happened in those three years.

After I'd spread out the blanket Mama had given me and was bending to lay on it, I caught a glimpse of Natalie Page, a girl around my age who lived next door. She was standing out on her back patio watching me in a curious way. Natalie was in my grade at school, but I didn't know her as a friend. I knew who she was—everyone knew who she was—because she was pretty and popular, but we didn't hang out together. We had passed a couple of times in the halls and had waved to each other politely, in an obligatory way, like neighbors do.

She smiled and waved when she realized I saw her watching me and I waved back. She turned and went into her house, and I stretched out on the blanket, letting the warmth of the morning sun caress my face.

Around noon, I started to get hot. The skin on my face stung and felt tight. I pulled one end of the blanket over my body to shield it from the sun. Mama must have seen me, because she knocked angrily on one of the windows facing the backyard to let me know she did not approve. I slung the blanket off.

She called the boys in for lunch and the yard got still and quiet, except for the chirping of birds. After a while, Nick came out and handed me a cheese sandwich wrapped in a paper towel and a small cup of water that I gulped down right away.

As I munched on the sandwich and listened to the birds tweet all around me, I decided I liked my new arrangement. Even though I was still confined to one area, being outside gave me a sense of freedom. It was far better than standing with my face to a wall in perpetual dread of what might happen to me next.

I stayed out in the sun all day and watched the sky change from blue to burnt-orange. When the sun had disappeared behind a distant hill, Mama called me in. She sent me directly to bed, telling me to sleep in the swimsuit, because I would be doing the same thing the following day.

When I woke up the next morning, I had sunburn on my face and all down the front of my legs and arms. My skin was swollen in patches and tender to the touch.

Mama took one look at me and said, "You may want to turn over once in a while so your back will match your front."

Like the day before, I stayed out in the yard on a blanket in the sun until late in the evening. Once again, that night I slept in the bathing suit. The next two days were the same.

While I was out in the sun, Mama fed me a lunch of a cheese, or peanut butter sandwich, but she gave me little to drink. After the fourth day of being out in the heat, I needed more water, so after everyone else had gone inside, I crept up to the house and snuck a drink from the dog's water bowl, an old metal pail under the outside faucet. A slimy brown film lined the inside of the bowl, but it didn't matter to me. I simply closed my eyes so I couldn't see it and sucked in the water. I was grateful for our dog, Rusty, when I was able to share his food scraps from the family's leftovers and now, as I plunged my face into his cool drinking water.

In the next few days, I drank from Rusty's water bowl every chance I got. But it wasn't enough. No matter how much I drank, I couldn't quench my thirst. After a week in the sun, I decided to try to slip into the bathroom at night and drink from the sink faucet.

After everyone else in the family was asleep, I jumped up from my bed and darted across the hallway into the bathroom. At first glance, Mama's white terrycloth robe, hanging from a hook on the wall by the tub looked like her standing there. I was so startled I wanted to run back to bed then, but I was thirsty, so I stayed on task.

Searching for something to hold water, I spotted, by the sink, a cup shaped like Mickey Mouse's head that held the family's toothbrushes. One by one, I took them out, and placed them on the counter. There were five of them, each a different color. The pink one I used to have before Mama got mad at me was now gone. It had disappeared like all of my toys had.

I put the empty cup under the faucet, and then cranked the cold water handle, carefully. The pipes made a rumbling noise when I turned the water on too much, so I had to dial it back to a slight dribble.

When the cup was full, I shut the water off before it splattered on the porcelain sink and made a sound. Then I turned up the cup and drank without stopping, forcing the water into my mouth so fast it ran in two streams down the sides of my neck. I filled the cup a second time, and a third to "camel up" for the next day in the sun.

When I ran back to bed, I could hear the water sloshing around in my belly and it made me laugh. I lay down to sleep, content with having solved my problem. Sneaking into the bathroom every night for water was doable, and with my thirst quenched, my days in the sun would be tolerable, which meant it was not going to be a bad summer after all.

29

By the end of my second straight week of lying in the sun, I became lawn furniture to the neighbors. The adults no longer paid any attention to me during their outdoor barbeques and the kids played around me as if I weren't there.

Under the blazing summer sun, the days melted together. Every morning before I went out, I wished for rain, or at least a sky filled with fluffy clouds that would, from time to time, draw a temporary shade over the yard, relieving me from the heat.

When I was blessed with an overcast day, I entertained myself by watching the clouds scud across the sky. Sometimes I imagined there was an enormous ballroom above me filled with beautiful women in elaborate party dresses with big, elegant hairdos, escorted by handsome men dressed in long-tailed tuxedos. Other times the clouds took on the shape of giant ice-cream cones, cotton candy and mugs overflowing with frothy root beer.

My mind was free to fill with wild fantasies. Out of loneliness I created my own imaginary friends, tiny elfin creatures with large, dark eyes and expressive faces. They lived under our house, where it was cool and damp and came out only when Mama wasn't around. As they huddled around me, I pretended I could feel the coolness radiating from their bodies, and it soothed my burning skin.

My imaginary friends were loyal and devoted only to me. They hated Mama for the way she treated me and together we plotted ways we might stop her from hurting me anymore. The elves suggested we tie her up and torture and starve her and when she begged for something to eat, we would force spoiled food down her throat. They even offered to kill her for me; all I had to do was say the word. But I couldn't allow them to hurt my mama because I loved her and I was still hoping that things would get better between us.

I had almost dozed off when I became aware of something blocking the sun above me. "Hi Tuesday!" said a female voice.

I could tell the slight figure standing over me was a kid, but I couldn't see who she was through the glare of the sun. I propped myself up on one elbow, craned my neck and shaded my eyes with my hand. I saw it was Natalie, from next door.

"Hi," I said.

"Mind if I lay out with you?" she asked. But she didn't wait for an answer. She proceeded to unfold a colorful patchwork quilt and spread it out on the ground beside me. "I have *got* to get some sun before school starts," she rattled on as if we were the best of friends. "I can't believe how tan you are; you look great!"

I glanced down at my body. My skin had turned a deep apricot that was striking against Mama's turquoise bathing suit. I smiled shyly. "Thanks."

Natalie stretched out on her quilt, leaned back on both arms and shook her long hair back away from her shoulders. She was wearing a pink one-piece swimsuit with white polka dots. Looking at her, I felt self-conscious of the one I had on, because the top was puffy where I wasn't yet. I reached up and tried to flatten it out with my hand.

"Sure is hot today," she said.

"Sure is," I agreed.

Grandma Storm had taught me it's not nice to stare and I tried not to, but I found it difficult. Natalie was so perfect. I had never seen her close up before and had not had the chance to appreciate her delicate, doll-like features. She had a smattering of freckles across the bridge of her tiny nose and eyes the color of the sky behind her.

"You make me look like a ghost!" She scooted off of her blanket and onto mine, until she was right beside me, our hips and legs touching. "Look how dark you are compared to me!" she said in a high-pitched voice. "And your legs are prettier too, so long and shapely."

My chest swelled with pride and an unexpected grin spread across my face. I couldn't have stopped it if I wanted to.

She reached beside her for a brown bottle of lotion, screwed off the cap and squeezed an extra-large dollop into her palm. "What are you using?" she asked, smearing the lotion onto her outstretched legs.

I had no idea what she was talking about. "Using?"

"You know—suntan lotion—what kind do you use?"

"I don't use any suntan lotion."

"You don't use lotion and you're that tan?" She offered the bottle to me. "Want some of mine?"

I glanced up at the house, wondering if Mama was watching us, then nodded and took it from her. I squeezed a dab into my hand and rubbed it on my legs. It smelled delicious, like coconut and bananas.

For an instant, as we lay there on our blankets, side by side, without Mama around to tell me I was ugly, or other kids to judge us, it almost felt like we were the same. Like she wasn't the most popular girl in school and I wasn't the scuzziest. It felt like we were equal and for an instant we were.

Natalie had been in the sun for only a few minutes and already the skin on her forehead sparkled with perspiration and the sprouts of baby hair framing her face were curling in the humidity. Her cheeks and nose had started to burn. She flopped around restlessly on her blanket. Then she sat up, pulled the top of her bathing suit out in front of her and blew air down her chest. "Whew!" she said. "How do you stand it out here every day for so long?"

She thought I stayed in the sun because I wanted to. Why would she think otherwise? I shrugged my shoulders.

I didn't want Natalie to go home and leave me alone. Somehow, her being with me made me feel more normal. I tried to think of something clever to say so she would forget about the heat and stay out a while longer. "I like your bathing suit."

"Thanks!" she beamed, squinting against the sun, a dimple deep in one cheek.

A few minutes went by. I couldn't come up with anything else to talk about.

All of a sudden, she leaped to her feet. "I just thought of something," she said. "I'm supposed to go with my mom to the grocery store. I almost forgot!" She gathered up her blanket and lotion. "Bye, Tuesday!" she called out as she unlatched the fence gate and headed for her house. "I'll see you later."

My heart sank as I watched her hurry up the slight hill of her yard. When she ran, her hair rippled in dark waves down her back. Right before she disappeared into her house, she turned around, flashed a smile and fluttered her fingers.

30

The following day the clouds were sparse and transparent and they floated across the sky like ghosts. Despite the heat, I noticed I wasn't sweating anymore. Usually after only a few hours in the sun, my body was covered in fine beads of moisture. It pooled in my navel until it overflowed, and then trickled down the sides of my waist. But on that morning, I was all dried up, like a slab of meat someone had forgotten and left burning in the oven.

My thirst had reached a new level. My mouth was now void of any moisture and my tongue felt thick and heavy. I had been unable to drink from the bathroom faucet the previous night because I was unusually exhausted when Mama called me in and had fallen into a deep sleep right away, not waking until morning.

Everyone was inside their houses because of the heat. The only sound was the white noise from the air conditioners running in unison. I searched the yard for movement, but it was dead still all around me. A haze of dust lingered in the air near the basketball goal, from earlier in the morning when my brothers had been playing before the heat set in.

Rusty slowly waddled over to his drinking bowl and took several laps of water. Panting heavily, he plopped down in the shade near the house, pressing his back up against the concrete foundation. Briefly our eyes met in empathy.

Desperate for water, I decided to sneak over to his bowl. I didn't like to drink from the dog's water in the middle of the day for fear of someone seeing me. But no one was around and I was so thirsty, I didn't care. I tried to get up to crawl across the yard to the bowl, but my body wouldn't move. The steady drip of condensation from the air conditioner hypnotized me and caused me to forget my plan.

The compressor kicked in and I snapped out of it. Suddenly I sprang to my feet, as if something had taken possession of my body, and started walking toward the house with a purpose that was unknown to me. Although fully aware of what was going on, I had no command of my actions. I simply followed my body as it moved forward—floated forward—not knowing where it was taking me.

I passed Rusty and his water bowl without stooping to drink and opened the back door to the house. Boldly I made my way through the forbidden kitchen without hesitation, past the place in the hall where I always stood, straight into my mama's bedroom. Disorientated, I stood there before her with a strange sense of calm.

"What are you doing in here?" she asked.

I opened my mouth, but could not speak and even if I could have, I couldn't tell her why I was there because I didn't know.

All at once, a dark tunnel formed between us, with Mama's infuriated face far away at the end. She was saying something to me; I could see her lips moving, but I couldn't hear her. She started coming toward me through the tunnel, tumbling around and around inside of it. The closer she got, the more the blackness engulfed her, until it had swallowed her up altogether.

As I drifted out of consciousness, it occurred to me that I was probably dying and I was okay with it.

When I woke up, Mama and my two oldest brothers were standing over me.

I couldn't move. *Am I dead? Is my family looking down at my lifeless body in a casket?* Then I recognized some of the objects in the room around me and knew I was in my bed.

Mama had an open book in her hand. She looked baffled. She began to read aloud from the book. "The person with heat exhaustion feels weak and dizzy. The skin is hot and dry and there is no perspiration..."

She and my brothers, along with the furniture in the room, began spinning around me. Every muscle in my body began to cramp.

Mama continued reading from the book. "There may even be fainting and convulsions..."

Against my will my legs and arms started pulling in close to my body, contorting out of control.

Jimmy D. interrupted Mama's reading. "Why is she jerking around like that?"

"I don't know, honey. Hush up for a minute and let me find out," she said. "Pour cool water over the victim. Wrap his head in cold, wet towels and his body in a cold, wet sheet. Give him cool water to drink..."

She stopped reading, put the book down on the bed and then disappeared from the room. When she returned, she had two wet towels and as the book had suggested, she bent down over me, close—closer than she had been since I was eight without hitting me—and wrapped me in the cool towels. As she placed one across my forehead, I could feel her breath brushing across my face and smell the floral fragrance of her perfume.

Finally I stopped jerking long enough for her to pour salty-tasting water into my parched mouth. I was thirsty and wanted to swallow, but every time I tried, my throat constricted. She gave up on the water and instead squeezed the moisture from a wet washcloth into my mouth.

The rest of the day and well into the next, I remained lethargic, drifting in and out of sleep. Mama came into my room regularly to feed me ice cubes to suck on, until I could tolerate water from a glass.

The second night, during one of those vague, blurry periods in between my coherence, she sat on my bed and spoke to me in a low, breathy voice. "I'm sorry for the mean things I've done to you," she said. "I love you and I always will."

I wanted to respond, but I was too tired. I tried to tell her I loved her too, but no words came out of my mouth.

Late the next morning, I awoke feeling well again. Mama brought me some ice water and chicken noodle soup with crackers crumbled up in it. As she handed me the cup of soup, I searched her face for a sign that she had changed, hoping she would follow up on the words she had whispered to me in my sleep the night before.

"Well, you look much better today," she said.

"I feel better!" I said happily.

"Well, in that case, I think it's time you get up out of bed and quit being so lazy. After you eat this soup, I want you to clean the house. You can start by sweeping in here." She turned and left the room without mentioning anything about the night before, as though it had never happened.

Maybe it didn't happen, I thought. *Maybe I dreamed it.*

For days I tortured myself, wondering if Mama in a moment of weakness and guilt, had broken down and revealed dormant emotions for me, emotions she might not have even known she had. I couldn't bear the thought that I might have missed the only chance I would ever have with her, or even that I allowed a few stolen moments of closeness between us to slip by.

31

Mama decided to put me to work pulling weeds around the chain-link fence in the backyard.

Pull them up by the roots," she yelled from the door. "Then beat the roots on the ground to get all the dirt off. I'll be out to inspect later."

It had been a while since the weeds had been tended to; they were about two feet high and the thick roots were all tangled up in the fence. Looking around our big yard, I knew the job was going to take the rest of the summer to finish, if I did it the way Mama said.

Grabbing as many weeds as I could hold in two hands, I tugged with all my might, but they wouldn't budge. I kept tugging until I lost my grip and fell backwards and the weeds sliced through my fingers. This happened again and again leaving my hands swollen and covered with long, diagonal cuts.

From time to time, Mama allowed me to stop and take a drink from the outside water hose, so I wouldn't dehydrate again, and I was thankful for this. But I was still weak from the heat exhaustion just days earlier. The weeding was tough work and I wasn't making much progress.

I hadn't been working long when Natalie walked up. She had on bright yellow hot pants and a white tee shirt with a shiny plastic daisy on the front. She still didn't have the tan she wanted, but I noticed the sun had coaxed out more of her freckles.

Breaking a smile, I said, "Hi!"

"Can you believe it's already time for school to start again?" she asked, even more effervescent than usual. "Aren't you excited?"

"I guess."

She pulled my arm. "You're still dark!" she said. "Want to come over to my house and play records in my room? I want to show you the new clothes I got for school."

"I—I can't."

Her eyes flashed blue sparks. "Why can't you?"

I shook some dirt clods from a handful of weeds I had just pulled. "Mama's making supper and she will be calling me in soon," I lied.

Natalie scanned the yard, as if a solution might be out there somewhere. I cringed when she looked in the direction of my pee-stained mattress that Mama had made me carry out to air that morning. She turned to me. "Can you come over tomorrow then?"

"No, I've got to pull weeds tomorrow too," I said. "I have to pull them every day until I finish."

She traced around the perimeter of the yard with her finger. "You mean you've got to pull *all* these weeds!"

"Yep."

She darted her eyes back to me. "Are you in trouble or something?"

"I guess so."

"What for?"

Just as I was trying to come up with an answer, Mama's radar detected what was going on and she poked her head out the back door. "It's time for you to come in now," she said with forced politeness, aware of Natalie's presence. "Supper's ready."

I headed for the house and Natalie walked with me. "Hi, Mrs. Storm," she said, as we approached Mama.

Mama threw up her hand and then went back inside.

Overnight, blisters the size of dimes formed on the pads of my hand from pulling weeds. When I resumed working the next morning, they popped open, oozing bloody pus.

I was both surprised and pleased when Natalie came out early and offered to help me with the weeding. She was hoping that if she helped me, I would finish sooner and then I could go to her house and play records. Selfishly, I didn't bother to tell her she would be wasting her time.

We worked side by side pulling the weeds together. She didn't seem to mind the way I smelled, or that you couldn't tell the bruises from the dirt on my legs. And she never once mentioned my funny haircut or the out-of-style clothes I always wore. She knew about the bedwetting too; she'd seen my mattress airing in the backyard. She looked past all these things as if they did not exist.

She wasn't much help with the weeding, though. She tugged and tugged at the stubborn weeds, trying her best to loosen them, but she wasn't strong enough to pull them up by the roots, like Mama had instructed. I had to go behind her and do it for her. But still, I was glad for the company and flattered that she was willing to work so hard to get to play with me.

When Mama saw Natalie helping me, she called me inside.

"You think that pretty girl really likes you?" she sneered. "Girls like Natalie don't hang around scuzzy kids like you. Believe me, Weasel, I know. I was just like her, one of the pretty, popular ones and I wouldn't have been caught dead with someone like you. She probably doesn't have anything else to do. As soon as she gets a big whiff of you, she won't get around you anymore."

I knew I smelled awful and sometimes I even got sick of myself. I swallowed back my tears because I didn't want her to know how much she'd hurt my feelings. I thought if only I was pretty like Natalie, it would solve everything.

Mama sent me out front to pick up gravel and rocks from the yard and throw them back into the driveway. As I squatted and pried rocks out of the dirt with my fingernails, I hoped Natalie didn't see me and try to help again. I liked having her around, but it was too much trouble concocting excuses why I couldn't go over to her house and play, and the real reason was too embarrassing to reveal.

I looked up and down the street at all the neat two- and three-bedroom brick ranches that lined Maplewood Drive. Each house had a picture window, under which was a flowerbed. In spring they were full of blooming pink tulips and buttercups, and in the summer, red or white geraniums. On Halloween a smiling jack-o-lantern could be seen burning on every front porch, and at Christmastime, live Scotch pines with multi-colored lights shone brightly through the windows.

Our house blended right into the tidy row with all the others on the street. The only thing that set it apart was the front door. All the other doors had windows that were square, triangular, or diamond-shaped. Ours was the only one with three rectangular windows in a diagonal. At night, Mama turned on the amber-colored hurricane lamp she kept on a table by the front door so the light would shine out through the three windows. She said it made the house look homey from the outside.

From a glance, you would never have guessed what went on inside our house. Only if you had paid careful attention as you passed by during your Sunday afternoon drive, or while walking your dog in the evenings, would you have been able to recognize the subtle ways in which number 1905 was different. For instance, even on a warm spring day, when all the other houses on the street had open windows with sheer curtains billowing in the wind, our shades were always drawn, and the doors tightly shut.

Natalie's mama, Lana, sat on her front porch step chatting with a lady from across the street. She was holding her youngest daughter, Katie, in her lap. Lana was a striking woman with a good figure—tall, thin and full-busted. She stirred the hormones of some of the pubescent boys in the neighborhood; they hid behind the bushes by her house and watched her sunbathing in her bikini. She was the reason Daddy rarely went out into the backyard anymore. Mama had once liked Lana, but since the accident she had become crazy jealous of her. She called her a slut behind her back and said she wore too much makeup.

Mesmerized by Lana, I watched her twirl a ringlet of Katie's hair around her finger as she talked. She smiled at me and threw her hand up when she saw me staring. I wondered if she thought it was strange that I was digging up rocks while all the other kids in the neighborhood were playing.

As far as I knew, no one who lived on Maplewood Drive ever questioned why I didn't play outdoors like my brothers. As far as I knew, they never noticed the sadness in my eyes and the hollowness of my cheeks when they saw me taking out the trash or pulling weeds. Everyone was too busy with their own happy lives and too intent on minding their own business. Their laughter was too loud during their afternoon barbeques and family games for them to hear the strange, bumping sounds and the muffled cries that sometimes came from within house number 1905.

That night I took the image of Lana holding Katie in her lap to bed with me and played it over and over in my head. I dreamed of what it would be like to be held by Mama again, to have her caress me and fondle my hair, like she once had. I wrapped my arms around my shoulders, closed my eyes and pretended she was hugging me and that she loved me as much as Lana loved Katie and Natalie. I held on tight until sleep took my worries away.

32

After school started, I didn't see much of Natalie. She hung out with the popular crowd, a group of girls who didn't know I existed. But whenever we passed in the halls, even when she was with her snobby friends, she always stopped to talk, if only briefly. She may have been nice to me out of pity, like Mama had said, but I didn't care. I was willing to accept her as my friend under any circumstances; she was that special to me. She had already given me enough of herself the past summer and I was happy to settle with whatever she had left to offer.

Things were looking up for me in the sixth grade. Daddy talked Mama in to letting me ride the bus to school, like my brothers. I was glad because it meant I wouldn't be late for class anymore. The kindness Natalie had shown me inspired me to make some changes to better my life. Instead of passively enduring Mama's humiliation tactics, I invented ways to counteract them. Like when she cut my bangs so short, they stuck straight out on my forehead, instead of facing the stares and snickers from my classmates, as soon as I got to school, I went into the restroom, wet my hair down with water and smoothed back my bangs, pinning them in place with some bobby pins I'd found while cleaning the house.

Natalie's friendship also sparked the confidence I needed to begin socializing with the other kids in my class. Some of them still made fun of me because I dressed funny, and—because Mama didn't let me take regular baths—sometimes I smelled funny too. Every morning I used the soap in the school bathroom to wash up the best I could, but there wasn't much I could do about my clothes. When the other kids made fun of me because of what I was wearing, instead of clamming up and sulking like I once had, I started laughing along with them. In doing this I discovered the teasing didn't seem to be as much fun for them and eventually they let up.

After a while, most everyone grew accustomed to my differences and some of the kids even decided to accept me in spite of them. A few friends were all I needed to make me start to feel better about myself.

Soon I went from being an introvert and not talking at all, to talking nonstop. By then I had figured out my life at home was going to be bad no matter what I did, so I thought I may as well have as much fun as I possibly could while I was in school. My deportment grades bottomed out, as I was always in trouble for talking too much. My scholastics fell below average too. I figured no one cared whether I made good grades or not, so what difference did it make? I liked art and creative writing and when I felt inclined, I excelled in those areas.

At home, the emotional cruelty remained consistent, the torture games sporadic and as usual, everything was unpredictable. The whippings I got while school was in session were usually on my bottom or my back, with a wire hanger, or the buckle end of a belt. If Mama became particularly mad, she hit me with her fist, but always where the mark wouldn't show.

As I matured, changes took place in my thought process. The delusions I'd held onto for so long—that my mama might forgive me and snap out of whatever was wrong with her—had all but vanished. I'd grown to resent her for making me suffer. I could no longer see her beauty. I could barely see her as human anymore.

At the beginning of the school year, I befriended a girl named Katherine Miller, who like Natalie, accepted me in spite of my appearance. She was a funny, free-spirited and independent girl, who didn't care what anyone thought of her. She was strong-willed too and stood for what she believed in and her every action was a bold, clear, testament to this.

The first time I saw her, she was in the lunchroom waving her finger at a couple of girls known for their cruel teasing and bullying. A boy whose name I didn't know was standing behind her, sobbing. I recognized the boy as an epileptic who had recently had a seizure in the hallway of the school. When it happened, he had foamy spit coming out of his mouth and his half-shut eyelids were fluttering. Some of the other kids were laughing and pointing and I could hear them saying words like mad dog and spaz. I remember feeling sorry for him, rolling around on the floor in front of everybody, his body jerking uncontrollably.

Katherine was not nearly as pretty as Natalie. Her eyes were large and bulbous and out of symmetry with her narrow face. She had bushy, brown hair that she wore long and parted in the middle and it draped her shoulders like a dark wool cape. I liked the way she looked, though, and I was glad she wasn't pretty, because being with her didn't make me feel self-conscious about my own flaws.

She was the ideal friend for me and in no time we were inseparable at school. Still, as close as we were, I couldn't bring myself to tell her about my life at home. What I wanted more than anything else was to be normal, to fit in and I thought if I ever revealed the truth, even to Katherine, there wouldn't be any chance of that happening. At the same time, all the unspeakable secrets inside me were clawing to get out.

Almost every Friday Katherine asked me to go to her house to hang out or spend the night. I put her off by making excuses, but there were just so many times you could have a stomach ache on a Friday. And I had run out of dead aunts' and uncles' funerals to attend.

"What's the real reason you won't spend the night with me?" she asked me one afternoon.

"I want to, Kat, I do, it's just that…"

"You still pee in the bed, don't you?" she teased. I had forgotten I had once told her I wet the bed as an excuse for not sleeping over. "Big deal! Don't worry; you can sleep on the floor. I'll put papers down like we did with our puppy before she was house-trained."

"That's not the reason I can't come over."

"Well, what is it then? We've been hanging out together every day since school started and here it is December and you haven't come to my house and I haven't been to yours one single time! We can't even talk on the dang phone because you won't give me your number!" She whipped her head to one side, slinging her hair back off her shoulders—Cher style. The hair-slinging thing was a nervous habit, a reflex, but there were times, like this one, when she did it in a cocky way, right after she'd made a good point.

I wanted to tell her the real reason why I couldn't sleep over at her house and my instincts told me she would understand and still accept me as her friend. But Daddy had warned me that if I ever told anyone about what Mama did to me, it could break up the family.

"Honey," he had said, in his most serious voice, "it's important not to talk to people about what goes on in the privacy of our house—you know, about your mama's illness and all. Let me handle it, I'll decide what's best for everyone."

At one time, I had believed every word he said and my faith that he would come through for me kept me from talking. But I had since learned his promises were a big load of crap and I had grown intolerant of him condoning Mama's cruelty toward me. The blind loyalty I once had for him no longer existed. I'd become fed up with my situation at home I was ready to try to find a way out. I decided it was time to tell her.

"It's my mama," I stammered, searching my mind for the right words. "She's—she's weird."

Kat rolled her bug eyes. "So is mine; who cares?" she said. "You don't have to bring her with you. Just ask her if you can come over."

In spite of the seriousness of what I was trying to tell her, she had me laughing as usual. "I can't just *ask* her." My voice squeaked from frustration. I hadn't thought of how difficult it would be to explain my situation. "You're not getting it, Katherine. My mama won't let me come!"

She laughed at me.

"She hates me, okay!" I blurted.

She kept laughing. She thought I was kidding. She didn't think it was even possible for a mother not to love her own daughter. "She doesn't hate you; she's your mother, for God's sake. Do you want me to have my mom call her and ask her if you can spend the night?"

"No!" I gasped.

Appearing frustrated, she put one hand on her hip. Her eyes were popping out even more than usual. "Well what do you want me to do then?"

"Nothing, there's nothing you *can* do." Then I said, in the most severe tone I could muster, "I'm serious, Katherine, my mama really hates me."

Kat studied my face carefully and then said, "You are serious, aren't you?" She dropped her hand off her hip, and her voice softened, "You *do* think your mom hates you."

"I don't just think it, I know she does!" I said as loud as I could get by with in school. "She tells me almost every day."

"Why?"

"Well, it started when my half sister, Audrey, got sick with the flu…"

"Whoa, whoa, whoa," she said. "You have a half sister? You never mentioned anything about a sister. You said you had three brothers."

"I *had* a half sister, but she died."

"How'd she die?"

"I killed her."

"What?"

"Well, I didn't exactly *kill* her, but it was my fault she died."

"Your fault, how?"

"I gave her the Hong Kong flu, and it killed her."

"That's not your fault!"

"Yes, it is. I was sick and I let her chew some bubble-gum right from my mouth and she got sick too and then she died."

"Wait a minute, something doesn't sound right here. I had the Hong Kong flu and I didn't die."

"She had polio and her lungs were weak."

"Then she died of polio; you didn't kill her!"

"But I wanted her to die because I always had to take care of her and she got all of Mama's attention."

"I don't care what you *wanted*. Unless you got a gun and shot her, or stabbed her with a knife, you didn't kill her!" She did her hair-flipping thing. "How old were you when all this happened?"

"Seven."

"For Pete's sake, Tuesday, you were a kid! Did your mama tell you she hated you because you killed your half sister?"

"No, she never said it like that. But she did tell me if I had never been born, Audrey would still be alive."

"It sounds like she's just hurt and looking for somebody to blame."

"Why does she tell me she hates me then?"

"I don't know. What does your dad say?"

"He thinks it's because of her head injury."

"Head injury?"

"She fell down the stairs not long after Audrey died and got a bad concussion."

"But it happened when you were seven, four years ago. She should be healed by now."

"That's what I thought, but Daddy said the doctor told him that with an injury to the front of the head, there was a possibility she could have a permanent change in her personality."

"I'm not a doctor or anything, but you would think she'd be better by now."

"I don't know whether it's her head, or what I did to Audrey, or both that made her start hating me and I've gotten to where I don't care. All I know is I can't take it anymore, Kat."

"How bad is it for you at home?"

"Bad."

"How bad?"

"Well, every afternoon when I get home from school, Mama makes me stand with my face turned to the wall. And I'm never allowed to talk, unless she asks me a question. I don't get to eat what everyone else in the family has; usually I get fat meat, or hog jowl and sometimes she doesn't feed me all day!" I watched Kat's eyes grow round. "Sometimes she hits me in the stomach and in the back with her fists as hard as she can, or beats me with the wire end of a flyswatter, or a broom handle, or a vacuum cleaner hose. Once she held my head under scalding hot water and…"

Kat waved her hands to stop me. "Okay, okay. Why didn't you tell me this before?"

"I was ashamed to tell you. I mean, it's awful! And I didn't want you to think something was wrong with me because my own mother doesn't love me. I was afraid you wouldn't want to be my friend anymore."

"Well, that's just silly. Why would I stop liking you because your mother is a mental case?"

After I had calmed down, I regretted having confided in her. Even though she assured me it was nothing to be ashamed of and kept saying over and over that it wasn't my fault, I was afraid she would tell someone and people would find out what a freak show my life was. I begged her not to tell a soul, even her mother and made her swear on our friendship she wouldn't.

"We've got to go now; it's time for class," she said, grabbing my arm. "We'll figure something out later, I promise."

I believed her; I had more faith in her than I did anyone, more than I had in myself.

33

It was early one morning, a couple of weeks before Christmas and I was on the bus on my way to school. As the driver pulled up the hill in front of our house, I noticed all the festive decorations our neighbors had put up. On one of the rooftops, bright against the pale winter sky, was a giant cut-out of Santa Claus with his team of reindeer. Another house had silver and gold bells strung across the gutter and twinkly white lights around the windows. On Natalie's front lawn, was a nativity scene, and her door was covered in glossy green paper with a huge flocked wreath hung on it.

At our house the decorations had gone up the night before: a wreath on the door, plug-in candles in the front windows, and of course, the tree. Mama insisted on a live tree every year because she liked the scent of pine to fill the house. My brothers had trimmed the tree, stringing it with large multi-colored lights and a garland made of cranberries and popcorn. They hung on shiny red, glass balls and real candy canes and then finished off with angel hair. Mama and Daddy looked on, sipping spiked eggnog and listening to corny Christmas songs on the record player.

As the bus geared down in front of Birch Street—the street Kat lived on—I cleared away the frost from the window with my coat sleeve and as I did every morning, looked out to make sure she was there at the bus stop. She was, and she had on a new red sock hat with a white furry ball on top. Her breath was curling in front of her face and she was bouncing up and down on her toes to keep warm.

She and everyone else around me, was obsessed with the spirit of the approaching holiday. The kids on the bus wore silly sweaters with snowflakes on them and prattled incessantly about what they were going to get for Christmas.

"You remind me of an elf in that stupid hat," I said to Kat as she walked onto the bus.

She sat beside me, took off her hat and hit me with it. "You're a sourpuss," she said, folding the elf hat in half and laying it in her lap.

Earlier that morning, on my way out the door to catch the bus, I had swiped two peppermint candy canes from our Christmas tree and stashed them in my backpack. I got them out and gave Kat one. She peeled part of the cellophane from it, bit off a tiny piece and then covered the rest back up and stuck it in her purse for later. I opened mine halfway, and sucked on it like a lollipop.

In the weeks after I had told Kat about my life at home, it became the main topic of most of our conversations. Together we wracked our brains trying to find an answer to my problem. After much discussion and deliberation, we could only come up with one solution. Kat thought of it, but I liked the idea, so it became "the plan." I was going to run away from home and live with her. All we had to do was work out the details of when, and how and then put our plan into action.

"What is Christmas like for you at home?" Kat asked.

"It was great before Mama's accident, but now it's terrible."

Kat rolled the peppermint around on her tongue a few times, and then stored it in one of her cheeks. "Do you ever get any gifts?"

"They put a few things out on Christmas morning, socks or underwear, sometimes a school dress. But I think it's so my younger brothers will believe in Santa Claus. When Grandma Storm was alive, she gave me dolls and all kinds of neat toys, but I never got to play with any of them. Mama always took them away."

"What a witch!"

"Two Christmases ago, a birthstone ring in a black velvet box was beside my usual school dress and socks. I got to keep the clothes, but Mama took the ring."

"Why?"

"Later, Daddy told me he had bought the ring for me without her knowing and it had made her mad, so she refused to let me have it. Last Christmas the same ring showed up again, but she took it away, and I haven't seen it since. I'll probably get it again this year."

"What's the point of giving it to you if you don't get to wear it anyway?"

"I don't know! I can't figure it out either, unless it's Daddy doing it behind Mama's back."

Kat fidgeted with the ball on her sock hat. "Tuesday, you said you didn't want me to feel sorry for you, but I can't help it," she said. "You know, my Aunt Jesse, the nurse, was over at the house and I asked her if an injury to the head could make somebody go nuts, like your mom. She said she has heard of some people who were never right again after a concussion. She called it a front lobe injury, or something like that. Tuesday, I believe your mom is nuts and maybe she can't help it, but you've still got to get out of there before she kills you."

My throat tightened, choking off the words of gratitude I wanted to say. I didn't want her to see the tears in my eyes, so I turned toward the window for the rest of the ride, fighting to keep from breaking down in front of all the kids on the bus.

When the driver pulled up in front of the school to let us out, I noticed someone had written "Merry Christmas" across one of the classroom windows with spray snow. I tried to recall what it felt like to have a merry Christmas.

34

Christmas morning I awoke to the sound of Ryan running down the hallway toward my parents' bedroom. "Mama, Daddy, get up!" he squealed. "Come see what Santa brought me!"

There had been a time when I awoke early on Christmas, like Ryan, eager for the rest of the family to get up. But I had no reason to be excited anymore. I no longer believed in Santa Claus and in the years since Mama had become angry with me, I received far fewer gifts for Christmas than my brothers.

Mama used to claim the reason I didn't get as much was because Grandma Storm gave me more presents than my brothers. It was true, she did, but she had good reason to. She was closer to me. After all, I spent my summers with her. And I think she knew—although she never wanted to talk about it—that I wasn't treated the same as my brothers. She was trying, in her own way, to make up for that.

Every year, when my presents from Grandma Storm and Aunt Macy arrived in the mail, Mama threw a fit and she and Daddy got into a major fight. "It's just not fair," Mama would say. "I'm not going to let her have all of this! How do you think it makes the boys feel?" Then she would take my presents away and put them somewhere before I even had a chance to open them.

When Ryan came back up the hall, Daddy had joined him. Mama was dragging behind, sleepily. She paused in my doorway. "Come on, Weasel, get up."

After having been let down so many times before, I decided I wasn't going to get my expectations up this year. But as I followed her, listening to my brothers tearing into their presents, I couldn't help but hope it might be the year when things would be different.

And it was.

When we got into the living room, Mama instructed me to sit on the floor in an area near my presents: the usual school dress, and for the third year in a row, the birthstone ring. I knew better than to touch anything without permission, so I sat quietly watching the boys play with their toys.

"Don't you want your Christmas presents?" Mama asked.

"Yes."

"Then act like it!" she shouted.

"Rose, not on Christmas," Daddy said. Then he turned to me. "Tuesday, why don't you try on your new ring?"

I fixed my eyes on the ruby stone nestled in the velvet box, but I was too afraid to pick it up. "Go ahead," Daddy said. "It's okay."

My hands trembled as I slipped it on my finger. I looked up at him and he winked, right in front of Mama.

I'd never paid much attention to the ring before. I hadn't wanted to become attached to it, because I knew Mama would only take it away, but now that it was on my hand, I drank in every detail. It was beautiful in its simplicity—emerald cut, rich red stone, flanked by two gold fans. I knew right then, as I admired it sparkling on my finger, I would never own a ring that would shine any brighter.

35

It was a month after Christmas, on a Saturday evening. The house was filled with the yeasty smell of frozen pizzas baking in the oven. Jimmy D. had invited a friend over to spend the night and upon his request, Mama was making pizza.

She was in the kitchen setting the table with paper plates and cups. I was sitting on the living room floor, within her view. Because we had company, I didn't have to put my face to the wall, but I still couldn't have the run of the house. She had given me a book to read—a collection of short stories by Edgar Allen Poe—so I wouldn't seem too conspicuous.

I was happy that night because we had company and Mama always put on appearances for company. Although I knew she would not go so far as to invite me to eat at the table with everyone else, I was sure she would bring me a slice of pizza to keep Jimmy D.'s guest from getting suspicious.

Being in the living room brought back memories of Mama's accident. Nothing had changed since that night. Nothing in the entire house had changed since then, except Mama. I tried to recreate the image of how I last saw her before it happened, curled up on the sofa asleep. It was too painful to even think about.

I turned my attention to my favorite part of the room, a nineteenth-century painting near the front door. It was of a woman—a Southern belle, according to Mama—seated in front of an intricately carved ivory vanity. On the vanity were bottles of perfume and bejeweled boxes overflowing with extravagant jewelry. The belle appeared to be getting dressed for a ball or some other grand event. She had on a teal green off-the-shoulder evening gown with layers upon layers of tufted satin. Her brown hair was short and wavy and from her reflection in the vanity mirror, I could see she had smooth, fair skin and dark eyes.

Standing behind the belle, also facing the mirror, was a black woman wearing a blue and white print dress with a white apron over it. A red bandana was tied around her head. She was on the plump side, with cheeks as round and shiny as polished apples. Her gentle, smiling face was that of a caring soul, the quintessential mother, someone who would always make sure you had plenty to eat and a safe, warm place to sleep.

The belle was fascinating to me, and as any young girl my age would have been, I was intrigued by her beauty and apparent wealth. But I was most drawn to the black woman, to her obvious benevolence and the tenderness in her face, and even though I was well aware that she was only a one-dimensional image in a painting and may not have even existed in any form other than in an artist's mind, I fell in love with her. I loved her because I perceived her to be kind and strong and righteous. I gave her life—a personality and a name. I called her Mattie.

There had been times when, on my way out the front door to catch the bus, I had looked up at the painting, closed my eyes and wished with all my might that Mattie was real so I could run to her and find safety in her layers of fat. She would gather me up into her arms and protect me from Mama. "Don't you dare touch this child again!" she'd say. And Mama would back off, terrified.

Mama called out for the boys to wash their hands because supper was ready. I could hear them running through the house and then splashing in the bathroom. When they had finished, they all went into the kitchen and shuffled around the table to get a seat, while Daddy cut the pizza. Soon they stopped talking and started eating.

About five minutes passed. I wondered why Mama hadn't brought me a slice of pizza. I thought she had forgotten about me, so I tried to make some noise. I crinkled a page of the book in an attempt to attract her attention. She didn't notice. I coughed a couple of times, still nothing.

Jimmy D.'s friend asked him why I wasn't eating with the rest of them.

"She doesn't like pizza," Mama said. "She only likes the crust and she's waiting for us to finish the rest of it."

That was when I made my decision. "I'm leaving tonight," I whispered to Mattie. And she smiled at me to show her approval.

After everyone else had finished eating, Mama brought me a couple of pieces of hard pizza crust and I gnawed on them as I planned my escape. I thought of Kat and how surprised and elated she would be to see me. I pictured the shocked expression she would have and enjoyed an inner laugh.

Daddy and the boys went back down to the den to watch television and Mama sent me to bed for the night. From behind my closed door, I listened for her to retire to her room. I had to make my move fast; I couldn't wait for her to go to sleep, because I didn't want to arrive at Kat's house too late. My adrenaline pumping, I pressed my ear to my bedroom door and listened to make sure no one was around. When I thought the timing was right, it took me less than five seconds to grab my coat from the closet, dash down the hall through the living room and out the front door.

As soon as I stepped out onto the porch, the winter air bit my face and sucked all the breath from my lungs. But I pushed forward across the front yard. I didn't even stop to zip my coat; I just pulled the hood up, held it together with one hand and raced up the street toward Kat's house.

To keep my mind off the cold, I focused on the sound of the frozen grass crunching under my feet. The rhythm of my running made me aware of my progress and reminded me of my goal. When I had topped the hill of Maplewood Drive, I turned back and took a final look at the house. The light from Mama's hurricane lamp in the foyer shone through the windows of the front door, casting three amber shadows out into the darkness. I zipped up my coat and tied the strings of my hood snugly under my chin. The coat was a few years old and the sleeves were too short. Whenever I had the hood on, it pulled my arms out away from my side. I giggled, remembering the time Kat had told me I looked like a penguin, and then without any doubt, or fear, I turned the corner and headed for Birch Street.

Kat lived only about four blocks from me, but by the time I had reached her street my chest was burning from running and inhaling the cold air. My breath hung heavy in white puffs in front of my face and stayed there until the next one came up behind it and pushed it out of the way.

Once I had Kat's house in my sight, I felt safe enough to slow down and walk the rest of the way. My heart pounding, I stepped up onto the front porch and rang the bell. Kat opened the door. When she saw who it was, the disbelief on her face far surpassed what I had envisioned it to be.

"Tuesday, what are you doing here?" as I had expected, were the first words out of her mouth.

"I did it! I ran away, like we planned."

Her jaw dropped. "You did not!"

"Yes, I did!"

"No, you didn't, you're teasing."

"Katherine, have you ever known me to come to your house for a visit?"

Her big eyes got bigger, bulged more. "Oh my God, you ran away from home!"

"It's freezing out here," I said, chattering my teeth. "Can I come in?"

She pulled me inside by my coat sleeve. The house was warm and I could smell wood burning in the fireplace, and food lingering from supper.

"Who is it?" Kat's mother hollered from the den, which was off the foyer.

"Tuesday Storm," Kat said. "I forgot to tell you she was coming over."

"Hi, Tuesday," Mrs. Miller said, walking into the foyer. She looked like a grown-up version of Kat. They even had the same hairstyle. She was wearing a long, new-looking red robe, probably a Christmas present. "It's nice to finally meet you!"

"We're going up to my room," Kat said, pulling me along behind her by one of my arms.

"Okay, have fun!" said Mrs. Miller.

The carpet in Kat's room was dark-blue shag and the walls were a lighter blue of the same shade. The shabby furniture, which was painted white, was chipped in places and some of the glass knobs were missing. Hair ribbons and yarn hung over one corner of the mirror above her dresser. On the other corner were strings of colorful beads and necklaces of all kinds. The rest of her jewelry—chokers and rawhide friendship bracelets—was in a pink and white music box, with a tiny ballerina inside, almost exactly like the one Audrey had.

Instantly I felt comfortable in Kat's room; I pulled off my coat, kicked off my sneakers and hopped on the bed among stuffed animals and fuzzy blue pillows.

"You stay right here," said Kat. "I'll go down and tell my mom you're spending the night with me. I'll tell her I forgot I had invited you. She won't mind."

A few minutes later, Kat popped back into the room. "Everything is cool for tonight," she said. "We'll deal with tomorrow, tomorrow."

It was still early, so we took advantage of our time together. We played our favorite songs on her record player and danced and sang along into a hairbrush. When we grew tired of singing, Kat styled my hair in two ponytails, while we looked at teen magazines and swooned over pictures of David Cassidy. Later we pigged out on hot cocoa and homemade chocolate chip cookies. It was well past midnight before we fell asleep in her bed, as if we didn't have a worry in the world.

The next morning Kat and I slept in until we got hungry and had to go downstairs to find something to eat.

When we walked into the kitchen, Kat's mom was pouring herself a cup of coffee. "Good morning, girls," she said cheerfully, like Grandma Storm used to. I wanted to run up to her and hug her, but I didn't. "Tuesday, I'm so glad you could sleep over last night."

"Thanks for letting me stay, Mrs. Miller," I said.

"Katherine has wanted you to come for a while. She talks about you all of the time."

I smiled at Kat, who was filling our bowls with Alpha-Bits.

"You live over on Maplewood, don't you?" Mrs. Miller asked, stirring sugar into her coffee.

I nodded.

"Do you need a ride home later? You shouldn't be walking in such cold temperatures. It's supposed to drop way below zero tonight."

Kat answered for me. "She's going to stay until this afternoon, if that's okay. Her mom and dad are going out of town today, but they'll probably pick her up later."

"That's fine," Mrs. Miller said. She breezed by us on her way to her bedroom, leaving a powdery smell behind.

Kat and I looked at each other for a second and then went on eating our cereal. Although we didn't say it, we both knew what the other one was thinking: we had not thought our plan all the way through, because neither one of us had believed I would have the guts to run away from home.

But I had run away from home, and there was no going back. Even if I wanted to, I couldn't, because my mama didn't want me there, and Daddy didn't care. I knew I wouldn't have to worry about them looking for me, because I was sure they were glad I was gone.

I slurped up the last of the milk in my bowl and followed Kat, who was in a hurry to get back up to her room.

"Okay," Kat said as soon as she had shut the door behind us. She did her hair-slinging thing, this time because she was nervous. "Before I can ask my mom if you can stay here, I've got to tell her everything. But when I tell her you've run away from home, she's going to get mad."

"Well, don't tell her then," I said.

"If you don't stay here, what are you going to do?"

I sat on her bed and grabbed a pillow, holding it close to my chest. "I'm not sure. Let me think about it for a while."

Kat sat directly across from me. "Tuesday," she said, "it would have been better if I had told Mom about everything *before* you ran away, but you made me promise not to. If you could, like, go somewhere for a while and let me talk to her and then maybe come back a few days later..."

"I don't have anywhere to go. I can't go home, I just can't." I sounded pathetic and I wasn't trying to. "Couldn't you hide me somewhere?"

She glanced around the cluttered room. "In here?"

"No, outside in the garage or something."

"Don't you think it's too cold to be outside?"

"Not if I stay in your garage. You can give me a blanket and I'll bundle up with it. Please, it would only be for a couple of days, until you've had time to talk to your mom and ask her if I can stay here for a while."

She thought for a minute, and then gave in. "Okay, I guess."

We went outside and scouted around for a place for me to sleep. Kat thought the garage was too risky because it was so close to the house. There was an old shed out back; she said it would be better.

At about six o'clock, we decided it was time for me to go out to the shed for the night. I took a shower and changed into some of Kat's clothes suitable for me to wear to school the next day. She found a heavy blanket that I could cover up with and stuffed a chocolate moon pie and a bag of chips in a paper lunch sack in case I got hungry.

We waited until Mrs. Miller was cozy on the sofa watching television and then Kat announced to her that my parents had come to pick me up. I said my good-byes, like I was leaving to go home, but instead I circled around to the back of the house and went into the shed.

In about half an hour, it started to get dark and the temperature dropped. I covered up with the blanket to stay warm and sat on a concrete block. It didn't take long for me to get drowsy, because Kat and I had stayed up late the night before. Under the glow of a streetlight, I scoped out a place to bed down.

An old wooden door with a broken window was leaning up against a wall and I decided that under it would be the perfect place to sleep. I wrapped the blanket around me like a cocoon, covering as much of my face as possible, and then balled up on the floor, making sure the warmth of my breath was directed down toward my body. Sleep came easily.

A faint, scuffing sound woke me up. I opened my eyes to unfamiliar surroundings. But then I saw the broken glass of the door leaning against the wall above me and remembered where I was.

I peeked around the side of the door, and saw a light tracing across the floor of the shed. My first thought was that it was Kat checking on me. Then, I heard a man's voice. "She's not in there, I tell you. If she is, she's frozen stiff by now."

"The Miller girl told me she was in the shed, so let's have a good look around to be sure," another man said.

There was more scuffing, then one of the men called out, "Tuesday Storm, are you in there?" The noises got closer. "Honey, come on out now, it's time to go home. Your parents are looking for you."

Home? Oh, no! If I hadn't been wrapped in the blanket, I would have made a run for it. The only other option I had was to remain still and hope they wouldn't find me.

"There she is!" one of the men said. "There, under that old door!" I saw the door being lifted away above me. "Tuesday, are you okay?" he asked, shining a flashlight in my face.

Through the glare of the bright light, I saw two police officers standing over me. I wiggled loose from the blanket. Once I was on my feet, one of the officers took my arm with his black-gloved hand and led me out of the shed.

When I got outside, I glanced over at Kat's house, and noticed her living room light was on. I saw a shadow of someone parting the curtain and peering out of the window, but I couldn't tell if it was her or her mom. I hoped she wasn't in trouble.

"You shouldn't have run away like you did," the officer holding my arm said. "Your mother and father are worried about you."

"Don't you know you could have frozen to death?" the other officer asked.

Sensing he was the more sympathetic of the two, I turned to him and begged. "Please, sir, don't make me go back."

As if he hadn't heard me, he opened the door of the patrol car and motioned for me to get in the backseat. "It's time to go home now."

During the ride I didn't say a word, but my mind was full of questions: *How could this have happened? Why did Mama send the cops to bring me home if she hates me? How did they find me? How did they know about Kat?*

The police officers were quiet too. They didn't ask what was so bad at home to make me run away and sleep on the floor of a shed in below-freezing temperature. They didn't ask me anything at all.

36

Kat felt bad about having to tell the policemen I was hiding out in her shed. "What was I supposed to do?" she asked the next morning when she got on the school bus. "They said that if you were out in the cold somewhere you could die."

"That's okay, Kat; I don't blame you." I gave her a hug. "Why do you think my parents sent the police to find me when they don't care about me?"

"They had to do *something*. I mean, it had been two days," she said. "Think about it. What if you had frozen to death out in the cold? How would your parents have explained not looking for their own kid?"

"Guess you're right. But I wonder how the policemen found out I was at your house."

"Mom said they questioned the neighbors on your street and all the streets around it. Someone must have told them we were friends. They showed up at our house in the middle of the night, asking about you and Mom admitted that you had been there earlier. They figured I had to know something."

Through Kat, I found out Mrs. Miller was livid when she found out I'd run away from home. She told Kat she'd better have a good excuse for all that had happened. Kat said she was left with no alternative but to tell her mom everything.

Mrs. Miller didn't want to believe something so horrible could be true. Then she thought it through. She knew how much Kat believed in me and she trusted her daughter's judgment. But according to Kat, her mom was influenced most by something she had seen in me, something that had haunted her the entire day after we met. She described it as sadness in my eyes, a look she had never seen in a child's eyes before. Her instincts had already told her something was not right about me and Kat's words only confirmed what she suspected.

As I had thought, Mrs. Miller was indeed a mature version of Kat, in ways other than her outer appearance. She had the same fire and determination. While everyone else looked the other way, she faced the problem head-on, taking a step no one—not even my own family members—had the guts to take. She called Social Services.

Early the following Wednesday, right in the middle of a math test, the teacher came to my desk and whispered that Mr. Tanner needed to see me in his office right away.

Mr. Tanner was our school's principal, but I didn't know much else about him. I mostly acquainted him with a powerful and commanding voice over the intercom. I'd only seen him from a distance in the auditorium when he occasionally gave a speech and had passed him a few times in the halls. But even though I'd never actually met him, I was well aware of his importance and of the implications of being sent to his office.

When I got there, Principal Tanner was standing outside the door. He greeted me with a smile and it put me at ease right off. "Don't worry, Tuesday, you're not in trouble," he said.

"There's someone in my office that needs to talk with you." Then stepping aside, he put his hand lightly to my back and guided me into his office. The kindness of his gesture made me, for a fleeting second, want to turn to him and throw my arms around him. But before I had the chance to do something so stupid, he shut the door, leaving me alone with a lady I'd never seen before.

It was the first time I'd ever been inside the principal's office; I had only peeped in curiously as I passed by on my way to class. Up close, Mr. Tanner's burgundy leather chair and cherry wood desk, stacked high with papers, were more intimidating than they had appeared from the hallway.

"My name is Mrs. Blackburn," the lady said, pulling two wooden chairs from a row of four that were lined up against the wall. She positioned the chairs facing each other and sat in one. "Have a seat, Tuesday. I'd like for the two of us to talk for a while, if that's okay with you."

The air in the room was close and it smelled of a mixture of leather and coffee. My stomach turned. I had no clue what was happening, but something told me it wasn't good. I didn't feel like sitting. I was too nervous and afraid. I wanted to turn and run from the office. But because the lady had the authoritative advantage of an adult, I did as she said.

Mrs. Blackburn was small-framed and she had mousy brown hair that she wore in a pixie cut. Her face was plain and free of makeup, with no distinguishing features. The kind of face you forget. A pair of black, cat-eye glasses hung from silver beads around her neck and a small black notebook lay neatly in her lap. In a soft, polite voice, she told me she wanted to ask me a few questions.

I nodded my head in agreement, as if I had a choice.

"Tuesday, why did you leave your home last week without telling your parents where you were going?"

The question made me feel like I was in trouble, like I had done something wrong. "Because I didn't like it there," I said.

"But your parents were worried about you. Didn't you care?"

"I don't know."

"Your parents provide you with a place to live and food to eat. Don't you think they deserve some respect for that?"

I was confused. I couldn't understand what she was getting at. "I don't know, I guess so."

"Tuesday, you told your friend, Katherine Miller, some awfully bad things about your mother. Why did you do that?"

"Because it's all true."

"What's true?"

"My mama treats me bad. Sometimes she does mean things to me."

"Like what?"

"Like hit me."

She put on her glasses and wrote something down in her book. I strained to read it, but it was too far away. Then she leaned in, narrowed her eyes and peered down at me through her glasses, suspiciously. "Tuesday, all children get spankings," she said. "Did you get mad at your mother because she spanked you? Is that the reason you ran away from home?"

I tried to look into her eyes, but the sparkling rhinestones around the outer edge of her glasses distracted me. So did the dust particles floating in a slant of sun behind her. I clenched both my fists. "No, I didn't run away just because she spanks me. It was because of all the mean things she does to me."

"Why don't you tell me what your mother has done to you besides give you a spanking? Tell me everything you told your friend, Katherine."

I was afraid if I told her it wouldn't help my situation and when Mama found out, I would be the one to suffer the consequences. Even if I wanted to tell her, I didn't know how. It had been hard to find the words to tell my best, most trusted friend in the whole world. How was I supposed to tell a stranger, a stranger I'd just decided I didn't particularly like?

I uncurled my fists to allow my sweaty fingers to air. To keep from looking at Mrs. Blackburn, I inspected my hands. They were shaking and I had squeezed my fists so hard, my fingernails had left indentions in my palms. Then all of a sudden an idea popped into my head, a possible way out of the predicament I'd gotten myself in, a way I could tell her without actually saying the words. "Didn't Mrs. Miller already tell you?" I asked.

"Yes, she did, Tuesday, she told me some things, but I need to hear about them from you." Her cat-eye glasses slipped down the thin bridge of her nose. With one quick shove of her forefinger she pushed them back up again. "You see, it's very important that you tell me how your mother treats you because it's my job to make sure that children are safe in their homes."

As soon as she said "safe in their homes," I started bawling. She stopped talking, but she didn't try to comfort me. She simply sat back and let me cry for a while.

"How can I help you, Tuesday, if you won't tell me what's wrong?" she asked, in a much more sympathetic voice.

Help me? Is she really here to help me? I wondered. My crying tapered off, and I managed to say, in jerky fragments, "My... mama...really...does...hate me."

She pulled a folded pink tissue from her purse and offered it to me. "Sweetheart, your mother doesn't hate you. Mothers don't hate their little girls."

I took the tissue from her and wiped the snot from my nose with it. "She does too! You don't understand! She beats me with a wire hanger and makes me eat gross things. She even tried to drown me once!"

The corner of one of Mrs. Blackburn's eyes started to twitch. It was the only indication that she had been moved by what I'd said. She reached over and pushed back a piece of hair that had fallen into my face. "Well, I'll just have to go have a visit with your parents, won't I?"

The thought of her talking to Mama excited me and scared me at the same time. "When?" I asked.

"Soon," she said. She got up and opened the door to the office, and with the same gentle nudging Mr. Tanner had used, helped me out the door. "Very soon."

For the rest of the morning, I couldn't concentrate on my schoolwork. My mind was like a scrolling marquee with thoughts trailing through continuously: *Am I going to be placed in a foster home? Will they take me away right after Mrs. Blackburn talks to my parents? Will they put Mama in jail?*

When lunchtime rolled around, I was too upset to eat in the cafeteria. The idea of being a part of a loving family elated me, but the dreadful occurred to me too. What if Mama talks her way out of it and I'm left to suffer her revenge? I knew she would surely make me pay and pay big for telling.

Then I remembered Daddy would be there to talk to Mrs. Blackburn too and I felt better, because even though he hadn't gone out of his way to help me like he'd promised, I just knew if the opportunity presented itself he would come through for me.

Mrs. Blackburn wasn't fooling around. By the time I got home from school, Social Services had already contacted Mama to set up a meeting. Mama must have called Daddy and told him what happened and he decided to take off work early. When I walked in, they were both sitting in the living room discussing "the problem." They had been drinking. I recognized the fruity smell of Southern Comfort, their favorite alcohol.

"Why did you do this to us, Tuesday?" Daddy screamed. "I told you not to tell anybody. I told you I would handle it!" The veins in his neck popped out. "Do you realize what you have done? Do you know I could lose my job over this?"

Before I could say anything, Mama turned to Daddy and said, "Whoa, whoa, wait a minute. What do you mean *you told her* you would handle it? When did you tell her this?" I was relieved that the heat was off of me.

Daddy fired right back at her. "Rose, do you want to argue, or do you want to take care of this problem?"

"You're right, Nick," she said. Never before had I known her to be so submissive.

Daddy faced me again. Three wavy lines were etched across his forehead and his green eyes had turned stormy gray. "What did you tell the lady from Social Services? I need to know what we're dealing with before she gets here. And she's coming at four thirty on Friday." He raked his fingers back through his hair nervously. "What did you tell her?" he snapped.

"Nothing," I mumbled.

"Nothing!" he bellowed out, and I nearly jumped out of my shoes. "If you had told her *nothing,* she wouldn't be coming here to talk to us!"

I knew I was in serious trouble; I started crying.

Mama sprang to her feet and said, "Shut up, or I'll give you a reason to cry!"

"Tuesday, I'm only going to ask you this one more time and you'd better answer me or else." Daddy's anger sounded more contained, but a new, deep-purple blood vessel that ran from his jaw clear up to his hairline, was now bulging. "Exactly what did you tell the lady who came to your school today?"

"I told her the truth!" I blurted, surprising myself with my boldness. "Everything!"

Mama was pacing the floor between Daddy and me. I could tell she was about to blow because of all the attention I was receiving from him. It didn't matter that it was negative; any interaction between us made her uneasy. When she couldn't take it anymore, she stopped in front of me. "Get out of our sight," she yelled. "Go to your room—now!"

I spent the rest of the evening in bed, listening to my parents' muffled, agitated voices in the living room. They talked well into the morning hours.

37

When I got in from school the next day, Mama sent me directly to my room. She brought me a plate of food for supper and sat it on the floor right inside the door. She was silent, and her movements were drone-like.

Again that night, she and Daddy stayed in the living room and talked, but this time in calmer, more controlled voices. I tried to listen in on their conversation, but they kept their talking low. I could only tell by their tone that they were not arguing.

Friday, when I got home, the house was clean and orderly and I could smell freshly percolated coffee. Mama was dressed in black slacks and a crisp white blouse and she had put on silvery frosted lipstick. Her hair was in a neat up-do and she'd even colored her roots.

Daddy sat solemn-faced in the living room, sipping a cup of coffee. The two youngest boys, Jimmy D. and Ryan, were cleaned up and seated beside him. Nick didn't appear to be home. When Mama saw me, she didn't say anything; she just pointed in the direction of my room and I knew what to do.

Before too long a knock rattled the front storm door. When I heard Mama invite Mrs. Blackburn in, I slipped out of my room and into the hallway so I could hear what they were saying. The knob was missing from the door leading into the living room and there was a small round hole, the perfect size for me to peek through without being seen.

After a brief introduction, Mrs. Blackburn sat in the Queen Anne chair by the front door. Mama and Daddy sat directly across from her on the sofa. Mama held Ryan in her lap and Jimmy D. stayed beside Daddy. They were all stiff, like they were posing for a family portrait.

Mama got up and disappeared into the kitchen to make more coffee, leaving Daddy to suffer through those first few awkward minutes alone with Mrs. Blackburn.

As Mama was coming back into the living room with the coffee, Mrs. Blackburn complimented the furniture and Mama's taste in decorating and everyone loosened up as they chatted about it. Then they made idle talk about the house, the boys and the coffee that continued for what seemed like a long time. Crouched in the hallway, I was getting impatient; after all, the meeting was supposed to be about me.

Finally Mrs. Blackburn sat her cup of coffee down on the marble-top table and opened the black notebook she had in her lap. It was her signal that it was time it get down to business. "As I told you on the phone, I came here to ask you some questions about your daughter, Tuesday. Where is she, by the way?"

"Oh, she's with a relative," Daddy said. "You said on the phone it would be best if she wasn't here."

Like she had done before when she talked to me in the principal's office, Mrs. Blackburn put on the cat-eye glasses.

As if they transformed her, she shed her friendly, conversational voice and assumed the same perfunctory attitude and tone she had with me a few days earlier. "As you already know, Tuesday ran away from home last week and went to a friend's house. Can either one of you tell me why you think she did this?"

"We think it was because she wanted to spend the night with her friend, Katherine and we wouldn't let her," Daddy said, acting as if he knew who Kat was.

Mama added, "Tuesday's grades haven't been very good this year and she's been getting low marks in behavior too, so she's been grounded from spending the night with any of her friends until she improves her schoolwork."

"I'm sure if you check with the school, they'd be glad to provide you with information about her grades to back this up," Daddy said.

"And you've discussed this with her?" asked Mrs. Blackburn.

"Oh, many times," he said.

"Well, Mr. Storm, when I talked with your daughter a few days ago, she had a different story to tell," Mrs. Blackburn explained. "She told me some disturbing things about the way she has been treated here. If what she said is true, then she is the victim of serious physical and emotional abuse."

My pulse quickened. *At last we're getting somewhere.*

Daddy put his coffee down. "I don't know what she told you, but I can assure you there is no form of abuse going on in this household," he said with conviction, and then kissed Ryan on the top of the head for effect. "We have four children, Mrs. Blackburn; we love all of them dearly, and we try our best to treat them equally. We love Tuesday, but she *is* our most difficult child."

His words shot through my heart.

Daddy paused briefly, reaching for Mama's hand. "She's our only daughter, besides one who passed away. And because she's the only girl, I believe she sometimes feels left out. She starves for attention and in order to get it, she concocts these wild stories about being mistreated. She's done it before, but we have noticed it has gotten worse since Ryan came along. The more children we have, the less attention we are able to give her, so this is how she reacts."

I was sickened by what Daddy had said. I had long ago accepted his submissiveness to Mama and I had even abandoned my delusions of him doing anything proactive to help my situation. But I never thought he would go to such extremes to hurt me, never thought he would disregard my welfare and fabricate such a story to cover his own ass. He had never appeared weaker in my eyes than he did at that moment.

Mrs. Blackburn glanced down at her notes. "But the information Tuesday gave me was detailed, things the average eleven-year-old couldn't possibly make up."

Daddy gave a throaty chuckle. "But that's just it. Our daughter is not average; that's something else you might want to ask the school about. Tuesday is probably the most creative writer they've ever had. She's a good artist too, but the stories she comes up with in her writing are amazing."

"She is an exceptionally smart girl," Mama chimed in.

Mrs. Blackburn then turned her attention to Mama, directing the next question to her. "Mrs. Storm, for some reason Tuesday focused more on you during our conversation. You are the one she feels is mistreating her the most. Why do you think that is?"

Mama responded without hesitation, in the sweetest voice I'd ever heard her use. "I'm not sure, but I would have to say it's because I'm the one she wants the attention from most. Like Nick mentioned before, I had another daughter who died..."

Sympathy brushed across Mrs. Blackburn's face. "I'm so sorry," she said.

"Thank you. There's nothing worse than losing a child," Mama continued, now weeping. "What I wanted to say was that my other daughter, Audrey, contracted the polio virus when she was a baby and was almost totally paralyzed for the remainder of her life. She required a lot of special care and I had no other choice but to direct most of my attention—maybe too much—toward her. It's probably my fault."

"That must have been a difficult situation for you," Mrs. Blackburn said. Her face had softened, but I could tell she was still not convinced. "When I spoke with Tuesday, she became upset during our discussion and began to cry. What do you think was so painful to her?"

Daddy took over again. "She's not getting the attention she so desperately needs and that is very painful to a young child. We didn't know how serious it had become until she ran away. Rose and I have talked about it and we've since decided to make a conscious effort to give her more attention and also to get her some counseling to help her deal with her problems."

"I think that's probably a good idea. She seems like such a sweet child; I hate to see her in so much pain."

"We were hoping you could recommend someone," Mama was clever to say.

"As a matter of fact, I do have access to some excellent counselors and I'd be happy to put you in touch with one of them." Mrs. Blackburn jotted something down on a piece of paper in her notebook.

"That would be so helpful," Mama said.

Mrs. Blackburn tore the piece of paper out of her book, stood and handed it to Daddy. "I won't take up any more of your time today, but I'll let you know if I have any more questions. In the meanwhile, make her an appointment to meet with a counselor. Any one of those I wrote down would be a good choice."

Mama and Daddy both walked Mrs. Blackburn to the door. "Thank you so much," Daddy said. "We appreciate your concern, and we know you're just doing your job."

As Mrs. Blackburn turned to leave, I had a sudden urge to run after her, but from what had just happened I knew it was useless. Now, with both my parents against me, I didn't have a chance to be rescued.

While they were still standing in the living room foyer, Mama and Daddy embraced, pleased with the outcome of the meeting. Then they kissed full on the mouth and Daddy slid his hands down to Mama's behind and patted it affectionately.

Hearing my parents lie and seeing how easily Mrs. Blackburn had dismissed my situation—dismissed me—left me poisoned with despondency. That day marked the lowest point of my life so far. I was left with no expectations for my future, nothing to look forward to and with the nearsightedness of a child, the life I had known for the past three years—a life of loneliness and suffering—was all I could see in front of me. I went back to my room, got into bed and cried for the rest of the day.

38

After what happened with Social Services, I expected Mama to be furious with me and for my life at home to get even worse. I readied myself for the rough ride ahead. It never occurred to me that she might have to put on a front in case the people from Social Services were keeping a watchful eye on her.

To be safe, Mama slacked off on her physical abuse of me and my face-to-the wall days were over at last. She couldn't bring herself to allow me to wander about the house freely, though, or interact with the rest of the family. She had me spend most of my time in my room, out of her sight, so she wouldn't be tempted to fall back into any of her old habits.

The space between Daddy and me had grown broader than ever before. He no longer made an effort to interact with me in any way. If by accident we passed one another in the house, he turned his head so his eyes wouldn't meet mine. It was as if he was trying to pretend I did not exist, the same way he was pretending the problem with Mama didn't exist.

As he had promised Mrs. Blackburn, he arranged for me to start seeing a counselor once a week for half an hour after school. The counselor, Mr. Jacobs, was one of Daddy's old friends from his teaching days who owed him a favor.

Mr. Jacobs had disheveled, gray hair and he always wore white dress shirts with yellow perspiration stains under the arms. He was a chubby, pleasant-looking man with an endearing childlike quality about him that I liked. He wore whimsical ties with cartoon characters on them and he kept a collection of beanbag animals scattered around his office. For some reason I never understood, he threw one of them to me each week as soon as I walked in. Our conversations went something like this:

"How was school today, Tuesday?"

"Fine."

"Are you getting those grades up?"

"Yes, sir."

"Staying out of trouble?"

"Yes, sir."

"Good, good. Hey, is your older brother still playing football?

"Yes, sir."

"Tackle, right?"

"Yeah, that's right."

We talked this way for a few minutes, about how I was doing in school, or what a great man my father was and then he did paperwork the rest of the time, while I did my homework or watched television. These visits lasted only a couple of months, long enough to appease Social Services.

Kat and I remained friends throughout the rest of sixth grade, but things were never the same between us. Neither of us mentioned the night I ran away from home again. Although she never said it, I got the impression that her mom didn't want her to hang around me anymore. When the investigation from Social Services fell through, it appeared to everyone that I had concocted the whole story about Mama mistreating me, which made it seem like I was disturbed mentally. And the sad truth was I didn't care what anyone thought. I was filled with such hopelessness I couldn't find the will to defend myself, even to Kat.

She started hanging out with other girls, normal girls with whom she could have a social life outside of school. Over time, I watched her grow farther and farther away from me, until our friendship was reduced to waving to one another as we passed in the halls.

At the end of the school year, she had a slumber party at her house to kick off the summer. She knew I couldn't attend and her mom didn't want me there, anyway, but she still gave me a token invitation.

The night of the party, I lay in bed remembering when I ran away and how much fun I'd had at Kat's house. Our time spent together almost made it all worthwhile. I tried to imagine what it was like at her party. I could see the blue shag carpet and shabby white furniture in her room and the squealing girls in pastel pajamas dancing and singing and jumping on the bed. I could hear the music they were playing. I could almost taste the cookies.

39

My grandmother on Mama's side of the family called to invite us to her house for the Fourth of July. Mama didn't want to go because she didn't like such gatherings. But the boys did and now, with Audrey gone, she no longer had a good excuse for not spending time with her family. So after some pressure from Aunt Barbara, she gave in and agreed to go.

Mama had a strange, superficial relationship with her mother. Since the accident she had distanced herself from both her and her younger sister, Barbara. She was all flattery and smiles to their faces, but when they weren't around, she bad-mouthed them.

She had been close to her father, who died of a sudden heart attack not long after I was born. She often talked about how much she missed him. According to her, she had been his favorite and claimed her mother and Aunt Barbara had always been jealous and resentful of her because of it.

Mama's mother was nothing like Grandma Storm. She didn't cook much and she drank Catawba wine and went on dates with men who dressed in brightly colored polyester suits. She was one of those grandmothers who didn't want to be one, nor did she want to be called Grandma, or any form of the word. The grandkids all called her Mother, because that's what Mama and Aunt Barbara called her.

As soon as we arrived at Mother's house, Mama had me sit in a corner of the living room by myself, and told me not to move from the spot or talk to anyone. She told everyone there I was being punished for something bad I had done and to leave me alone.

My cousins didn't understand why I couldn't play with them. They pleaded with Mama to let me get up, but she wouldn't give in. "Go away and leave Tuesday alone," she said to them. "She's being punished for something—something dreadful."

"What did she do?" my cousin Eva, who was two years younger than me, asked her.

"Oh, Eva, it's so bad, I can't even talk about it." Mama said.

Eva sat on the floor beside me and crossed her legs and arms in front of her, Indian style. She and I could have passed for sisters. When we were toddlers, we looked almost like twins, but now that we were older, you could tell us apart by our hair. She'd kept her cotton top, while mine had turned a dirty blonde.

Eva looked up at Mama defiantly. "My mom said I could sit here with Tuesday and talk for a while."

"Oh, she did, did she? Well, if you want to give up your play time to sit with someone who's being punished, that's fine with me," said Mama, and then she joined Mother and Aunt Barbara in the kitchen.

My cousin, Bruce, Eva's older brother, who was my age, sat on the floor too, on the other side of me. I liked Bruce. He was sweet and shy. And although we barely talked to each other, I felt close to him. He was more concerned about Mama's treatment of me than my brothers were.

The three of us sat there for a while, without saying much, and then Eva moved closer to me. "What did you do wrong, Tuesday?" she whispered.

I didn't want to go into the whole story about the bubblegum and Audrey's death and Mama's accident. "I don't know," I said.

She leaned in. "Don't be embarrassed, you can tell me."

"No, I mean it, I really don't know. I'm always in trouble and I've never been able to figure out why."

"I know you are!" Bruce said. "Aunt Rose never lets you play with us and you've always got to sit on the floor all by yourself. I asked my mom why and she said she didn't know either."

"It's been that way since I was eight. I guess I'm used to it."

Bruce got up and went outside to join my brothers in a game of badminton. Eva stayed with me.

"What do you want to do?" she asked.

She looked up to me, probably because I was a few years older and I knew she would do almost anything I asked her to, so I took advantage of it. "They have any dessert in there?" I asked.

"My mom brought sugar cookies with icing—red, white and blue stars! Want one?"

"Sure! But you'll have to get it for me. Remember I can't get up," I said. "And you'll have to hide it from my mama too. She doesn't allow me to have sweets."

"How am I supposed to do that?" Eva asked.

I knew exactly what to do. I'd become a master at sneaking around and I had no problem giving her instructions. "Go into the kitchen and get a cookie for yourself. Then when nobody's looking, stick another one under your shirt and bring it in here to me."

Eva jumped up from the floor and ran off into the kitchen. A minute or two later, she came back, her shirt bulging in the front. She had the goods.

She brought me three cookies that day and stayed with me until we left. She even ate her meal right beside me on the floor, balancing her plate on her lap.

This aggravated Mama, but there wasn't a thing she could do about it, because she didn't have any control over Eva's actions. It delighted me to know she was not the boss of everybody.

My birthday came and went without a celebration, or a cake, or even a mention of the special occasion. But the rest of the summer was better for me that year, because Mama was trying to put on appearances for Social Services. Mrs. Blackburn was still dropping by the house now and then to check on how everything was going with me. Sometimes she didn't call first, so Mama had to make sure I was always cleaned up and fed, just in case Mrs. Blackburn decided to pay a surprise visit. On the days she knew Mrs. Blackburn was coming, she let me play outside; the rest of the time I spent in my room.

40

Whitmore Junior High had gray, drafty halls, high ceilings and exposed pipes. It was much bigger than grade school and I felt small and insignificant within the cold, concrete walls.

Never before had I seen so many kids together at once and I hardly knew any of them. I had hoped Kat and I would have some classes together in the seventh grade, but I was disappointed to find out we didn't. Every day I searched for her among the countless strange faces in the halls. Somehow we lost each other forever in the crowd that year.

Once I had adjusted to my environment, gradually I made some friends. School was my only contact with other people, so I thought in order to get them to like me I had to make an impression in the short time I was there. I did a lot of talking in class and often got into trouble for it. As a result, once again my behavior grades were not good and neither were my scholastics.

Aunt Macy had sent me a few cute outfits for my birthday the previous summer and I was surprised, but delighted, when Mama let me wear them to school. Mama also gave me a pair of her then-fashionable go-go boots, because I had outgrown all my shoes. For the first time, I was allowed to bathe regularly and I wore my dark blonde hair long, straight and parted in the middle, like most of the other girls my age. There was no longer a reason for the kids to tease me about my appearance.

Now a handsome young man had become the focal point of my fantasies, replacing the mean, dwarfish, creatures that I'd imagined had lived under our house on Maplewood Drive. The young man had black hair and dark, penetrating eyes. He was tall and strong, like Daddy, but unlike Daddy, he was not at all afraid of Mama. In my fantasies, he confronted her and laughed in her face, calling her crazy. He told her how beautiful and desirable I was and how old and ugly she had become. Then he picked me up, as I fell breathless and weak in his arms, and carried me away to his castle to be his wife.

That year I started paying more attention to the boys at school and my new look provided the dose of confidence I needed to start flirting with them. I had my first real boyfriend in the seventh grade, a shy, lanky kid named Jerry Stevens.

Except for being tall—the tallest boy in junior high school—his appearance was the direct opposite of my fantasy man. He had frizzy, white-blonde hair and pasty skin and if it weren't for the faint blue in his nearly transparent eyes, he might have been mistaken for an albino. I thought he was the best-looking boy in the seventh grade and I welcomed what others may have perceived as imperfections. To me, they were part of his appeal.

Because Mama still wouldn't allow me to go out socially to the skating rink or the theater like the other kids my age, Jerry and I only saw each other at school. Our relationship was limited to occasional, brief conversation in between classes and passing notes in study hall, which was the only class we had together. He was content, though, with the way things were and he never asked me any questions about my life at home.

Jerry rarely said anything at all and when he did talk it was about embarrassing and ridiculous subjects, like his ability to bite his own toenails off, or his talent for drinking milk and then blowing it out through his nose. Whenever he was around me and did get up the courage to say something, his face always went scarlet and he stuttered when he talked.

One day in study hall, he passed me a note asking me to meet him after class, because he had something he wanted to give me. I knew it could only be one thing—what all the guys gave their girlfriends—his ID bracelet. Only a handful of girls my age were "going with" somebody and only a select few wore their boyfriends' ID bracelets. I was so thrilled I could hardly wait for class to be over.

I spotted Jerry from far off in the hallway, his big pale head bobbing above all the other kids'. I made my way to him. He stood before me, red-faced as usual and smelling strongly of Brut cologne.

"What did you want to give me?" I asked him, coyly, pretending as if I didn't know.

"Oh yeah," he said, like he had forgotten and started fishing for something in the front pocket of his jeans. Hand shaking all the while, he pulled out and offered to me a shiny gold identification bracelet. "I w-was w-w-wondering if you w-wanted to w-w-wear this."

I tried to act cool, like it was no big deal, but I was about to burst. "Sure, I guess so," I said.

"D-d-do you w-want me to help you p-put it on?" he asked.

I extended my wrist to him, and he wrapped the bracelet around it, but his hands were shaking too much to fasten the clasp. "That's okay," I said after a few failed attempts. "I'll do it." I pulled back my wrist, took the bracelet from him and put it on. "I love it, Jerry! Thanks!" I gushed. "We've got to go now, or we'll be late for our next class."

As I walked down the hall on my way back to class wearing Mama's go-go boots and Jerry's ID bracelet, I held my head high, smiled and waved at all my friends as they passed. For the first time since I was eight years old, I felt like I was the same as everybody else.

41

My parents had been discussing the possibility of leaving Spring Hill ever since the incident with Social Services. But I never thought they were serious until toward the middle of my seventh grade school year, when out of nowhere, they announced we were moving to Kentucky.

Daddy had accepted a position as personnel director of a government-funded youth rehabilitation facility in a place called Uniontown, in Western Kentucky. His new employer wanted him to start right away. They agreed to furnish him and his family with a place to live free of charge until he found a suitable house in the area.

I knew Daddy's new job wasn't the real reason we were leaving Tennessee. We were leaving because ever since the incident with Social Services, Mama had become paranoid that people were talking about her. I heard her and Daddy arguing about it almost every night. Even though nothing more ever came of the report of child abuse, she still thought Kat's mom was talking bad about her around town and pressing for a more extensive investigation from Social Services. She wanted to leave the rumors behind her and start over somewhere else. She thought moving to Kentucky would solve all her problems.

I didn't want to move away from Spring Hill. I was happier there—at least at school—than I had been in a great while. I liked the new friends I'd made and I had a boyfriend who I was crazy about and he had just given me his ID bracelet to wear.

For Christmas that year, Jerry had also given me a gold bangle bracelet with delicate flower etchings on it. I kept it in my locker at school, and made sure I only wore it while I was there, because if Mama knew about it, she wouldn't have allowed me to keep it.

As soon as I found out we were moving, I brought the bracelet home, because I wasn't sure exactly when we were leaving and I didn't want to risk the chance of losing it altogether. I hid it under my mattress where I thought it would be safest and checked on it often to make sure it was still there.

One afternoon, when I got off the school bus, I saw a moving van parked out in front of our house. When I went inside to my room, I discovered my bed frame had been disassembled, ready for the movers to load on the truck, and my mattress was on the floor. Right away I remembered my bracelet and started looking for it. I searched everywhere, but it was nowhere to be found.

I wondered if maybe one of the movers had come across my bracelet and kept it, but I was afraid to accuse them. I couldn't say anything to Mama because I didn't want her to know about it and Daddy and I weren't even speaking anymore. There was nothing I could do but accept that my bracelet was gone.

The next day my brothers and I stayed home from school to help pack for the move. By early afternoon we were taking off for Kentucky.

It was only a four-hour drive to our new home in Uniontown, but it seemed like forever. Mama was always nervous having me in the car with Daddy and her boys. With six people in such close quarters, somebody had to sit by me and maybe even— God forbid—touch me.

The atmosphere in the backseat was grim. Nick and Jimmy D., who had been moping around for days because they didn't want to move away from their friends, were long-faced and they glared straight ahead of them as if they had lost all reason to go on living.

I was just as miserable. Every time I had to travel anywhere with the family, Mama made me sit on my hands and look out the window for the duration of the trip. Inside my heart was broken because I knew I would never see Jerry again and I had a sinking feeling my life was about to change, this time for the worse.

Daddy stopped at a traffic light beside a long blue car with two kids in the backseat laughing together. In another car I saw a mother passing out sandwiches and chips to her children. We passed carload after carload of happy families, and I wondered why ours couldn't be one of them.

As much as Mama had wanted to move, once we arrived in Uniontown, she immediately decided she didn't like it. Contrary to what she had expected, the staff housing where Daddy's employer had temporarily placed us, was not at all glamorous. It was a rundown, mice-infested modular home, well below the conditions she had been accustomed to. She was also concerned that because the house was located so near the rehab center where Daddy would be working, one of the "convicts,"—as she called them—might escape and murder, or rape her. From the outset, she griped constantly about how Daddy had failed her by dragging her to such a "godforsaken place."

Daddy was enthusiastic about his career change and quickly became preoccupied with his new job. Mama, with plenty of free time on her hands, started drinking more. Now that she was safely away from the ghosts she had left in Tennessee, she was slipping back to the way she was before Social Services had snooped around. She often got drunk and went off on lengthy rampages about how ugly I was and reminded me how much she and the rest of the family despised me. As if I could ever forget.

It was right around this time that she became fixated on certain physical features of mine. My lips were too thick. My face was bony. My hair was stringy. Sometimes, while I was eating or taking a bath, she would stand over me and pick me apart.

"I can't believe how ugly you are," she said one night while I was in the bathtub. "You have a horse face and you're such a bony ass. You don't even have breasts like most girls your age."

As a reflex I glanced down at my puffy, budding nipples. She was right; the girls I went to school with were already well-developed. Mama had gone through puberty early, starting her period at twelve, and Audrey had done the same. I was taking after the late bloomers on Daddy's side of the family. Near my twelfth birthday, she had left me brochures in my dresser drawer about menstruating, along with a box of sanitary napkins and a belt to keep them in place. I read the brochures, but the rest of the stuff was still unopened.

"There isn't one single pretty thing about you. I'm so ashamed of you and so is your daddy."

She got no reaction because I no longer cared what she or Daddy thought of me. She had said the same words so often, I had grown immune to them and they now rolled off me as easily as the bath water.

Still, she went on and on with her insults. When I ignored her, she said them at the top of her voice. When I didn't flinch, she said them vehemently.

"Your lips are too thick," she shouted. "I'm tired of looking at them. From now on, whenever you're around us, I want you to hold your lips in your mouth—like this." She pulled her own lips in, squeezing them tightly between her teeth to demonstrate.

I nodded my head, acknowledging that I understood.

"Do it right now!" she screamed, smacking me in the ear with the back of her hand.

Even when she struck me, I hardly felt the pain anymore. I had become numb, inside and out. I pulled my lips in, like she said and went on bathing. As soon as she left the room, I let them back out again.

In the middle of the night, Mama flung open the door to my room and tugged the string of the overheard light so hard, it snapped up and smacked against the ceiling. Startled from a deep sleep, I sat erect in bed.

"You're never going to have any boyfriends, Weasel. You *do* know that, don't you?" Her eyes were glassy and she smelled of alcohol. "Your brothers are ashamed of you. They tell me practically every day that their friends talk about how ugly you are and that you don't even look like part of our family." When she spoke, frothy balls of spit flew from her mouth. "Nobody is ever going to want to go out with you, let alone marry you."

She quit talking for a minute and examined my face. Finding no trace of emotional response from me whatsoever, she played her trump card. "Look what I found," she said, sticking one of her arms in front of me. "It was on the floor when we were moving out of the house on Maplewood."

At first what she had said didn't register. I was still half asleep and anymore I didn't pay much attention to her words. I blinked a couple of times to clear the sleep from my eyes. Then I recognized, gleaming in the light, my bracelet—the one Jerry had given to me for Christmas.

My initial impulse was to lunge at her and rip it from her wrist. I struggled to contain my anger. *You bitch!* I thought so loudly, I could have sworn I heard myself say it. But on the outside, I showed no indication of how mad she had made me.

"I love it!" Mama said, twisting my bracelet around and around on her wrist. "I think it may be gold. What do you think?"

In her eyes, I could see the insatiable need to hurt me. But I refused to give her the satisfaction she reached for. I kept my face set in stone.

My lack of emotion sent her into frenzy, and all at once she came at me, socking at my face with both her fists. Her movements were slowed by the alcohol, giving me time to duck my head and tuck my face close to my chest, forcing her blows to land on the top of my skull. I knew her knuckles hurt when they hit me. It was my retaliation.

She grabbed my hair and jerked my head from side to side, and then up and down. "I hate you, I hate you, I hate you," she screamed.

I hate you too! I screamed back at her. It was only in my head, but I know she heard me.

42

Once we were safely away from Spring Hill Social Services, Mama could no longer bring herself to let me wear clothes that flattered my figure. Her new mission became to make me appear as unattractive as she possibly could in front of my classmates at my new school. She took back the go-go boots she had given me and one day, the clothes Aunt Macy had sent me suddenly vanished.

All I had to wear to finish out my seventh grade school year were clothes left over from the sixth grade and I had outgrown most of them. The only thing I could still squeeze in to was a pair of green, polyester stretch pants. But even they were too short, hitting me about mid-calf. Mama decided I was going to wear them anyway and they became the foundation from which she built the rest of my wardrobe.

She dug out some of her outdated blouses to go with the pants. For shoes she had already stumbled upon the perfect solution while ordering work clothes for Daddy from the Sears catalog. They were men's boots, the kind that zip at the ankle. She ordered a pair in brown, two sizes too big so I wouldn't grow out of them anytime soon.

For a coat, she found an old one of hers from when she was in high school. Not only was it decades out of style, but it was also the ugliest coat ever made. It was faded brown tweed, with frayed sleeves, buttons the size of Frisbees and an oversized, floppy clown collar accented with wide black trim.

Getting dressed on the morning of my first day at Uniontown Middle School, I did the best I could with the clothes Mama had given me to wear. To make the polyester pants appear longer, I ripped out the hem and pulled them down as low as possible on my hips, so low the crotch was hanging just above my knees. And still, a three-inch gap was between them and the two-sizes-too-big ankle boots that made my feet appear comically large for my scrawny legs.

Mama drove my brothers to school, leaving me to ride the bus with a bunch of people I didn't know. Even though it wasn't cold outside, she saw to it that I wore the ugly clown coat out the door, but as soon as I got out of her sight, I took it off and stuffed it into my book satchel.

Approaching the bus stop, a cloud of dread hovered over me. I knew getting on the bus was not going to be a good experience. It was inevitable I would stand out as the new kid. A given I would draw attention wearing the low-hanging, short pants and hideous men's boots. And a guarantee somebody was going to laugh at me. But I had no way of knowing I was going to be the only white kid on the bus as well.

It started with one stifled giggle. Then some kid in the back hollered out, "Look at those high waters!"

A few more giggles erupted. They kept multiplying, rapidly, and getting stronger, each one feeding off the others before it, until the whole bus roared. I pretended I didn't know what they were laughing about and kept my head down, as I hurried to find a seat.

Uniontown, Kentucky, was a small, coal-mining town of hardworking churchgoers. It seemed as though all of them knew one another, bound together in some way, whether by blood or through singing together in the church choir.

The people of Uniontown were wary of newcomers. They had become comfortable with the sameness of their cozy world and anything different scared them. Even if I had dressed normal, been normal, the folks there probably still would not have accepted me, because I hadn't been born there. To them I was, and to a certain extent would always be, considered an outsider.

Uniontown Middle School, like any other school, had its popular crowd, the cheerleaders and football players and kids with rich parents. Nice clothes, with brand names like Izod and Aigner, were mandatory to get into this group. If you didn't have a brass *A* or an alligator somewhere on you at least three days out of a week, you had no chance of being one of them. The kids in the popular crowd didn't come anywhere near me, but they stared as I passed by them and sometimes there were whispers.

Most of the kids in school were from blue-collar families. Their fathers worked in the mines, like their fathers before them had. Within this group were all kinds of kids, including nerds and rebels—the wild ones who smoked and wore leather jackets. The kids in this group were too busy struggling with their own problems and insecurities to judge me. They were distantly polite.

Those remaining were the outcasts—the poor, the ugly, the ones with skin conditions, cold sores and bad teeth. They had been pushed from all the other groups, so they clung together forming a group of their own. They accepted me because they recognized me as one of them. I was at ease around the outcasts, particularly the ones who wore ragged clothes and I felt a kinship with the kids who were overweight, or had kinky hair and acne.

Although I was able to blend in with this group, I never could bond with any single one of them the way I had bonded with Kat. I was too afraid to try again to make a true friend, too afraid I would fail to pass beyond the soundness of the wall that isolated me from the ordinary world.

Every morning, on my way to the bus stop, I took off the clown coat and stuffed it into my book satchel so nobody would see me with it on. But one day it was so cold out, I absolutely had to wear it, or freeze to death.

I stepped onto the bus prepared for the worst and that's exactly what I got. The combination of the clown collar, the short pants and the oversized boots was too much for a busload of kids to handle. The laughter started the instant they saw me.

Looking around at all the gaping mouths and bobbing heads, I wanted to turn and run back out, but the bus doors clamped shut behind me.

Then a girl with caramel-colored skin and soulful brown eyes sprang from her seat. "Ya'll hush!" she yelled. "Maybe her mama and daddy can't afford no better." She tugged at my arm, directing me to the seat beside her.

She told me her name was Vanessa. I recognized her as one of the popular girls in school, a cheerleader. "Don't pay no mind to them," she said, smiling, her teeth as straight and perfect as the keys on Grandma Storm's piano. "They're just being silly; you look fine."

I was nothing to her, a stranger, the new kid, a weird one at that, and yet she had, without reluctance, stood up for me like I was her sister. What she had done both moved and mystified me at once. I did not know how to aptly express my gratefulness. I thanked her again and again, but it didn't seem like nearly enough.

From that day on, every morning and every afternoon, Vanessa saved me a seat beside her on the school bus. As long as I sat with her, the other kids didn't make fun of me as much. Like a lost puppy, I attached myself to her and when she got off at her stop, I wanted to follow her home.

43

After we moved to Kentucky, there were only a couple of instances like the one with the bracelet when Mama lost her temper and attacked me violently. Every now and then she slapped me in the face, or kicked me when she walked by, but nothing like when I was younger. Instead, she got her gratification, her need to punish me, from causing me to be humiliated in front of my peers and attempting to inflict emotional pain with her words of belittlement. But it seemed like no matter what she did, she simply could not get satisfied in her efforts.

The next idea she came up with was to stop letting me shampoo my hair. After only a few days of skipping shampoos, because my hair was naturally oily anyway, it became plastered to my head. After a week it hung in heavy clumps around my neck.

To me this was the worse humiliation tactic of all. I could take the clown coat off as soon as I got to school and when I sat at my desk, I was not so self-conscious about the pants, but there was no way at all to conceal my head from the other kids.

"That girl's hair is so greasy, you could fry an egg in it," a boy who sat behind me in my first period class said.

The girl who sat directly across from him commented, "I thought it was wet, like maybe she took a shower right before she came to school."

"No it's not wet, because I've got sixth period with her and it's still like that," said the boy.

"Why doesn't she wash her hair?" the girl asked. "Is she too poor to afford shampoo?"

"Either that, or she's not right in the head. She never talks to anybody, keeps to herself all the time."

"Wonder if she even takes a bath?"

"I don't know and I'm not going to get close enough to her to find out."

For a while, after hearing what the other kids thought of me, I sank into despair and spent many nights in bed, pining over my unfortunate life. After about two weeks of this, I realized my self-pity wasn't helping matters at all and my hair was only getting greasier. I came to the conclusion that I needed to take action to solve my problem because things were not going to get better on their own.

Instead of whining, I spent my nights wracking my brain for a solution until I came up with a plan I thought I could pull off. I was going to wash my hair under the outside water faucet one morning before getting on the school bus. Mama usually let me leave about ten minutes before the bus came and I figured that would give me just enough time to do it if I moved fast.

First I needed to steal some soap from the bathroom at home. But something so risky called for careful consideration and timing, as Mama continued to keep close supervision over me. In order to get my hands on a bar of soap, I had to slip out of my room during the night while she was sleeping.

The bathroom had only one bar of soap out for the family to use. I knew I couldn't take that one because she would miss it and I always got blamed for everything that went missing around the house. I would take a new one from the bathroom cabinet; it would be less likely she would notice it was gone.

After I got the soap, I decided to put my plan into action the following morning. It was exceptionally cold out, but I didn't let the weather deter me. I couldn't take another day of hearing the whispers and seeing disgust on the faces of the kids at school.

When I walked out the door on my way to catch the bus, without a minute to waste, I reached into my book satchel for the soap I had stolen from the bathroom the night before, and then ran around the side of the house to the backyard.

The instant I got to the faucet, I tossed my books on the ground, dropped to my knees and turned it on. I stuck one of my hands under the water first to check the temperature. It was cold all right, but I was too fired up to appreciate just how cold. And my time was limited, so I didn't have long to ponder the issue.

Taking in a deep breath and holding it, I put my hair under the running water long enough to get it wet. Immediately I felt my scalp go numb, and then my hands. I took the bar of soap, and rubbed it against my hair, vigorously, to work up lather. I rubbed and rubbed, but the soap just slid around on my head.

Off in the distance, I heard the school bus breaks screech when it stopped to turn off the highway into staff housing. I knew that meant I didn't have much time left to make it to the bus stop. Panic surged through my chest at the thought of missing the bus and having to stay out in the cold all day. I put down the bar of soap and stuck my head under the water again to rinse my hair.

When I heard the bus getting closer, I shut off the water, shoved the soap back into my book satchel and took off running full speed to the bus stop. When I was almost there, I reached up and tried to comb my hair out with my fingers. It was stiff on top because I hadn't rinsed out all of the soap and worse yet, it was crunchy on the ends where it had started to freeze.

As soon as I got on the bus, a girl hollered out, "High Waters!" It had become my nickname. "What did you do to your hair?" she asked. "Did you fall in the water you were wading in?"

Everyone busted out laughing, including the driver. With a hand that felt like a baseball glove, I patted clumsily at my head, trying to smooth out the pieces of my hair that were sticking up on top. "I was running late this morning," I said. "I just got out of the shower."

I searched for Vanessa's kind face and when I spotted it, I made my way to her and sat down in the seat she'd saved for me. She had to turn toward the window to keep me from seeing that she was trying not to laugh.

Vanessa didn't ask me why my hair was wet and soapy that morning, just as she had never asked me about the strange way I dressed. She didn't ask because she thought she already knew the answer. She thought it was because my family was poor. And I didn't tell her any different.

"You would be so pretty if you put on makeup and wore something stylish," she said. "Do you want to come over to my house sometime? I'll lend you some of my clothes, and show you how to put on mascara and eye shadow."

Of course I couldn't take her up on her offer, but her generosity alone touched a tender place inside of me that had only been touched once before.

Vanessa was the one person in Uniontown I knew I could trust with my secret, but I could not gather the courage to tell her. After what had happened with Kat and the fiasco with Social Services, all the disappointment and humiliation, I figured there was no use. Besides, with both my parents against me, I didn't stand a chance anyway and would only end up making a fool of myself again. So I trudged on from day to day, wearing my protective armor, trying to salvage the traces of my dignity that remained, doing the best I could with what I had available to me. But inside I could feel my breaking point was getting nearer.

At home, Mama had begun withholding food again. Some nights she didn't feed me supper and she often forgot to give me lunch money. Whenever I got the chance, I stole a handful of loose change from Daddy's nightstand and used it to buy lunch. On the days I didn't have money, I went to the cafeteria anyway and walked from table to table, shamelessly bumming food from kids I had never met.

This went on for a few months, until one day help fell from the sky like a heavenly gift. On the way to one of my classes, I passed the lunchroom and noticed something posted on the door. I stopped to read: "Wanted: Student Cafeteria Workers. Payment Is Free Lunch." I went right in and applied.

Most kids had no need to work in the lunchroom. The poor ones got their lunch for free anyway, so I got the job because no one else was interested.

The lunchroom work was easy. All I had to do was transfer the food from the pots to the serving pans and then help with the dishes. Not only did I get to eat free for doing this, but I could also have as much as I wanted. The ladies who worked in the cafeteria were amazed by the amount of food I could put away. They didn't know I was trying to store up enough to last through the night, in case Mama didn't feed me supper.

After stuffing myself with food every day, in a matter of months, my weight went from a puny one hundred pounds, to about one hundred and forty. My clothes started busting at the seams. Three rolls of fat formed on my stomach and my thighs rubbed together when I walked.

44

Finally Daddy located a house to suit Mama and we were able to move out of the modular home in staff housing.

Our new house had two roomy stories and a basement, much bigger than our place on Maplewood Drive. Nick was thrilled because he had been promised a room of his own when we moved. But because there were only three bedrooms, Jimmy D. and Ryan would still have to share one. My room was to be downstairs under the stairway in an area formerly used for storage.

It was an older house, built in the early 1900s. Mama's massive Victorian furniture fell gracefully into place in the grand formal living room, with its twelve-foot ceiling and crystal chandelier. All the original woodwork remained intact, as did many of the original light fixtures.

Although the new house was large enough for our family and it did have its antiquated charm, hardly anything had been done in the way of renovating. "There are plenty of things here to keep you busy this summer, Weasel," Mama said.

First she wanted all the baseboards, door facings and the molding around the windows to be hand-sanded down to reveal the grain of the original wood. Then I would strip the French doors leading from the living room into the dining area. The hardwood floors throughout the house, which had been heavily shellacked over the years, would be next.

While I did the work, she continued to monitor my every move, even to the point of sacrificing her own privacy and free time. She either sat right under me, or came in to check on me every few minutes.

We had been in the new house only a few weeks when it occurred to her that in such a big space, she wouldn't be able to watch me like she wanted to during the night. Her master bedroom was upstairs and my room was downstairs, too far away from hers for her comfort, and worst of all, right across from the kitchen. She was afraid I might sneak out at night while everyone was sleeping and steal their food, like I had before. And she was right.

She had to come up with a way to somehow keep me in my room, which meant she had to figure out how to lock my door from the outside. In search of a lock, she went to the local hardware store and came across the kind normally used on the inside of front doors to keep intruders out of houses. She bought one in the heavy-duty size, complete with a chain and built-in buzzer, designed to go off if the door attached to it was opened more than a few inches.

That night after supper, Daddy got out his tools and mounted the lock on the outside of the door to my room under the stairs. Then they opened the door over and over to see if the chain was sturdy enough, and the buzzer worked properly. As a final test, Mama went upstairs to her bedroom and Daddy set off the buzzer so she could be sure it was loud enough to hear if I tried to escape during the night.

My afternoons and weekends were spent working on the house. At night I was locked in my room under the stairs, where I ate my meals, when I got them, did my homework and spent the rest of the time reading books, until Mama made me turn out the light.

My new room was compact. At the most it measured six feet by eight, barely enough space for my bed to fit in. I was always bumping my head on the ceiling that slanted with the stairs above it and the closet had a three-foot-tall door that I had to stoop down to get into. It was stuffy too, because there were no windows or vents to circulate the air. The only light source was a bare bulb in the center of the room, and when it was turned off it was dark, even during the day. At night it was black upon black.

Despite its oddities I grew to love my room under the stairs. It became a tiny haven for me, a space where I could get away from Mama's anger and the ridicule I suffered at school. I would rather have been alone in my room than anywhere else.

The only problem I dealt with was where to go to the bathroom. During the week, I became good at retaining my bowels at night until I could use the restrooms at school the next day. Usually I could hold it on the weekends too, but there were a couple of instances when I had to go bad. So I did, on some notebook paper. Then I wrapped it in several more sheets of paper and stuck it in my book satchel until Monday morning when I tossed it in a Dumpster on my way to the bus stop.

My main problem was with peeing. Mama usually came and let me out to go once right before bedtime. But she often got busy and forgot. Once, when I couldn't hold it any longer, I went into the short closet, squatted near the back and went right on the floor. The pee soaked into the old, porous wooden planks and disappeared. I shut the closet door, certain that no one would ever find out what I'd done. I continued to do this whenever I needed to, confident I'd found a solution to my problem. What I didn't know was the pee was not disappearing at all, but seeping through the floor to the ceiling below, which was the area between the back door and the entrance to the basement.

It took Mama a while, but she finally figured out where all the yellow stains on the ceiling of the landing were coming from. She was infuriated. She knew she had to come up with some other way for me to go to the bathroom, or I would keep peeing in the closet and staining the ceiling.

So back to the hardware store she went. She returned with a metal bucket for me to keep in my room to use as a toilet. When she gave it to me she made it clear that it was to be used only for peeing. She permitted me to empty the bucket once a week, on Saturday, if she remembered.

After sitting for several days, the odor of the urine was beyond foul—almost unbearable in such a cramped space. When I breathed through my mouth to keep from smelling it, I could taste it. Sometimes I pressed my nose to the crack at the bottom of the door in an effort to suck in some of the clean air outside my room.

45

Before I knew it summer was upon me and I was worried. I didn't know how I would get enough to eat when I no longer had access to the cafeteria food at school. Thankfully Mama had plenty of work lined up to keep me busy and that meant more time out of my room, which meant more opportunities to steal food.

At the top of Mama's list of jobs was to move a huge coal pile from out of the basement. She wanted me to carry the coal scuttle by scuttle up the stairs outside to the far end of the yard and then dump it behind a shed. This was good news to me because a shower and toilet was down in the basement. Not only could I go to the bathroom and clean myself up every now and then, I would also have access to plenty of drinking water.

Early in the morning, on the first day of summer break, Mama issued the uniform she wanted me to wear to haul the coal: a pair of her bright pink knee-length pants—she called them pedal pushers—and a long-sleeved red and yellow plaid shirt that had once belonged to Jimmy D.

The clothes were another one of her attempts at humiliating me. She thought I would be embarrassed to wear them outside in front of my brothers and their friends. But she was spitting in the wind with that one, because I had long ago moved beyond the point of embarrassment to a place where such things didn't even faze me.

Every day, all day, I hauled the coal up from the basement, unless it rained. When it rained the basement flooded and this created a whole new job for me. Mama gave me a Mason jar to dip the water from the basement floor and pour it into a bucket. Once the bucket was full, I took it up the stairs and emptied it outside. Then I headed downstairs again to fill another bucket. As soon as the basement was dry I went back to the coal pile.

After a while, hauling the coal began to take its toll on my body. The muscles in my arms and shoulders ached deeply and I had a nasty bruise on the side of the thigh I used to support the bucket of coal as I carried it up the stairs. I was often weak because I never ate breakfast and rarely got supper. Usually Mama fed me once around lunchtime. But it was not uncommon for me to go an entire day without anything to eat at all.

At first I lived off the fat I'd gained from working in the cafeteria during the school year. But with limited food and all the exercise I was getting, it didn't take long for my ribs to start showing and my face to go gaunt again. Soon I had to fold the pedal pushers over twice at the waist to keep them from falling off. Even then they slid down my hips as I walked and I had to stop every once in a while, put down the bucket of coal and pull them back up again.

All day, I thought of nothing but food. At night I pressed my cheek to the floor to smell the evening's supper as it seeped from the crack under my door. Every time Mama passed my room I got anxious, thinking she might be coming to feed me. After so many of these nights lying awake hungry, consumed by thoughts of food, desperation took hold and I decided to break out of my room and steal something to eat from the kitchen.

The only way to get out was to conquer the buzzer lock on the outside of my door. Every chance I got I took a quick look at it, each time observing a different part, engraving every detail in my mind. First I studied the slotted groove that held the chain permitting it to slide back and forth, and then the length of the chain and placement of the notch that released it. I also took into consideration how high the lock itself was mounted on the door.

At night, I monitored the family's habits, trying to pinpoint the best time to slip out. Because my room was right under the stairs, I knew from their creaking when everyone went up for the night. I noticed once they were upstairs they rarely came back down again. They would lie in their beds and watch television until they fell asleep; every so often I heard footsteps across the floor when one of them got up to go to the bathroom.

When there were only a couple of buckets of coal left in the basement, Mama came down and made an announcement. "Nick and I have discussed it and we've decided to burn coal in the fireplaces this winter. So that means we're going to need all the coal moved back down here to the basement."

I could tell from the smirk on her face it pleased her to pass this information on to me. She thought the news would be upsetting and that I would be hurt to hear she and Daddy were still united against me. But I didn't care. I had long ago given up on Daddy. Actually I was glad I would be hauling the coal a while longer. The mindless work afforded me more time to think, more chances to study the lock and perfect my plan to break out of my room for food.

For almost two weeks, I traced over my mental image of the lock on my bedroom door before I felt confident enough to make an attempt to disengage it. With a determination driven by my hunger, I watched the family's shadows flit across the floor, waiting for them to disappear. Once they had all gone upstairs, I listened for their movements to end. When the house was silent and I was positive everyone was asleep, I proceeded with my plan.

In order for the chain of the lock to be released, it had to be slid across a four-inch groove and then pulled out through a notch. I figured I could do this with a wire clothes hanger, and had already put one aside that I had found in the back of the closet in my room.

I straightened the hanger out enough to reach the lock, but not so much that it would lose its stability, and then I shaped it into a slight arc so it would fit around the edge of the door. I left the hooked part of the hanger bent, adjusting it slightly so I could use it to grab the chain.

If I opened the door even a hair too much the buzzer would go off and I would be caught. Carefully I cracked it open about three inches. According to my calculations, that was as far as the chain on the lock would stretch without setting off the alarm. I stuck the hook end of the wire hanger through the crack, extending it around the edge of the door. Then directing the wire up toward the lock, I sought out the chain with the hook.

As I tried to slip the chain onto the end of the hanger, I breathed in the air outside my room. It was not stale like my air and did not stink of urine. It was warmer and smelled like food from supper and the soap from my brother's showers.

Suddenly these scents from their world sent the reality of what I was doing sweeping through me. Fear started at my toes and then shot up my body to the tips of my fingers like an electrical current. Visions of Mama coming down the stairs flashed through my head.

Despite my best effort, I couldn't get the chain to go onto the end of the hanger. After a while, I could no longer maintain the awkward position and had to retract my arm to rest it. Once I had regained my strength, I tried again, pressing my jaw firmly against the door facing, straining to see out as far as I could through the opening.

Hours passed, of failing to hook the chain, resting and then failing again. Finally I gave up and went to bed hungry and nail-spitting mad.

46

By the time I had finished moving the coal pile from behind the shed back to the basement where it was in the first place, Mama had another job waiting for me. She wanted me to paint the two wooden storage sheds behind our house. But first I had to scrape off all the old paint that was chipping away. With only a couple of weeks before school started back up, I figured it would be my last project of the summer.

The morning I started to work on the sheds, everyone in the family was outside, except Mama. Nick, now seventeen, was backing out of the driveway in his car. Jimmy D. and Ryan were pitching a baseball back and forth in the yard. Daddy, who had decided to trim some of the tree branches that had grown too close to the house, was rounding up the tools he needed for the job. When he had to walk by me to get the ladder out of one of the sheds, he acted as if he didn't see me.

I watched him drag the ladder across the yard and then prop it against a towering maple tree, extending it as far up the trunk as it would reach. With the chain saw in one hand, he slowly pulled his large frame up each rung of the ladder with the other. Once he had made it to the top, he wrestled with the cumbersome saw to bring it in front of him and then situated himself on one of the limbs.

He cranked the chainsaw, but the motor wouldn't turn over. He cranked it again. Still no luck. After he had pulled at the cord several times, it belched a puff of gray smoke and sputtered to a reluctant start. The raspy noise of the chainsaw apparently annoyed Jimmy D. and Ryan because they stopped pitching ball and headed for the house.

While I scraped the sheds, I rethought my plan to sneak out of my room for food. I focused on the lock on my door and the clear mental picture I still had of it. I knew it would be difficult to muster up the gumption to try again, to risk the chance of getting caught. But I'd made a promise to myself to not give up next time, no matter how tired I got, no matter how scared I became.

Out of the corner of my eye, I caught sight of something falling and looked over to see that it was a huge tree limb Daddy had just cut. It hit the ground hard with a loud crunch. The thickness of the wood had caused the chainsaw to stall, so Daddy cranked it up again and this time it started without a fight.

Smaller tree limbs continued to fall one right after another as he cut them, each one meeting the ground with the same crunching sound. After the first few, I became accustomed to the motion and the sound and the falling limbs no longer distracted me from my work.

After several minutes the chainsaw stopped again. I assumed Daddy had cut another thick limb, but nothing dropped to the ground. So I thought maybe he had finished trimming. I looked over to where he was and expected to see him coming down the ladder. When he didn't come down, out of curiosity, I looked up to see what he was doing. Before my eyes found him, they caught sight of red streaks on the tree trunk. I traced the color to Daddy's leg, where blood gushed forth in a steady stream from a deep laceration on the front of his thigh.

His face had lost its color. In his eyes, I saw fear and desperation—two things I'd never seen there before. No one was outside but the two of us. I was his only hope. If I didn't do something to help him soon he would die up there at the rate he was losing blood. Now he was the one who was helpless and I was the one who had the choice to either save him, or stand by and watch him suffer.

I ran up to the back storm door and banged on it with both fists. Mama appeared. "Daddy cut himself!" I screamed out, pointing up at the tree.

Right about then, Daddy dropped the chainsaw. His blood splashed from it when it hit the ground. Mama stared at the bloody saw, blankly. It took a few seconds before it registered in her mind. She stepped out onto the porch and looked up the tree to where Daddy was. When she saw what had happened, she ran back into the house screaming.

By this time Daddy was struggling to make his way down the ladder using one hand to put pressure to his wounded leg. Mama came back out with a stack of towels and the car keys. Jimmy D. and Ryan were on her heels. "We've got to get your daddy to the emergency room," she said, locking the house behind her.

She helped Daddy hobble to the car. "I'm too nervous to drive," she said, her voice trembling. "Where's Nick Jr.?"

"He's gone," I said. "I saw him leave in his car about thirty minutes ago."

Jimmy D., who was eleven at the time, in a wild act of bravado, got behind the wheel of the station wagon. "I'll drive, Mama," he said.

"You don't know how to drive!" She pulled Jimmy D. from the car. "Get in the back with your brother. I'll have to do it." She looked over at me. "You stay here, Weasel. If Nick Jr. comes home before I do, tell him what happened and that we've gone to the emergency room."

The wheels of the car churned gravel in the driveway as she backed out and sped away in a cloud of chalky dust. Beside me, at my feet, the chainsaw lay in a puddle of blood. Fragments of Daddy's skin clung to its teeth. There was a trail of blood that ran from the tree to the driveway, stopping where he'd gotten into the car.

When Mama was out of sight, I walked around the house to check and see if the front door was locked. It was, and so were all the windows. I couldn't get inside to get anything to eat, but I took advantage of the opportunity to drink from the water hose.

About three hours later, Mama returned. Nick Jr. pulled in the driveway right behind her. They stayed home long enough for Mama to lock me in my room and to gather some of Daddy's things. I heard her tell Nick Jr. that Daddy needed several stitches in his leg and had to be admitted into the hospital because of blood loss.

With no one home but me, it was the perfect time to try once again to unlock my door and get something to eat from the kitchen. I readied the wire hanger, double checking to make sure it was curved enough to make contact with the lock and then I opened the door and slid it through.

The hook of the hanger slipped easily into one of the links of the chain after only a few tries. Gingerly I moved the hanger forward, guiding the chain along the groove, while simultaneously closing the door as the tension increased. A couple of times I dropped the hanger and had to start all over again. But I worked with more tenacity than before, pressing on. Finally I heard the chain drop.

Easing open the door, I walked out of my room, my heart pounding against my chest so hard it hurt. It felt strange being free to roam about the house without Mama's supervision, and for some reason, even though I knew no one was home but me, I was still scared. For so long I had wanted nothing more than to unlock my door so I could sneak out and steal some food. But now that it was happening, all I wanted was to get it over with so I could return to the safety of my room.

When I got to the kitchen, my attention shot in all different directions. I looked in the pantry. There was so much to choose from—peanut butter, cookies and potato chips—I didn't know where to start.

I opened the refrigerator, and using my bare hands, stuffed my mouth with whatever I could grab: leftover fried chicken, mashed potatoes, and chocolate pie. I decided to eat as much as I could and then stash some food in my room for later. After I had filled my stomach, I grabbed a package of graham crackers, a jar of peanut butter, and a loaf of bread and headed back to my room.

Just as I got there, something dawned on me and I stopped in my tracks. I couldn't take an entire loaf of bread and a jar of peanut butter without Mama getting suspicious. I went back to the kitchen and searched the cabinet drawers until I found some plastic Baggies. I spooned peanut butter into one, spoon and all, and in another, I crammed several slices of bread. I thought it would be alright to take the whole package of crackers because there were still two more left.

Before I went back to my room, as a special tribute to Mama, I got out the orange juice from the refrigerator and raised it high in the air. "A toast to you, Mama," I said, drinking right from the carton. She was always afraid I would somehow "contaminate" her family with my germs. Then I gathered up the food and returned to my room.

Once the door was shut behind me, I felt safe once again and proud of what I had pulled off. It was when I was hiding the spoils of my effort under a loose floor plank in the closet that it hit me: *I have to lock the door back!* I had been so concerned with getting it unlocked I hadn't studied on a way to lock it back again.

My hands shaking, I got the wire hanger, hooked the chain onto the end of it and then shut the door as much as I could. The problem was, as I tried to move the chain toward the notch, it kept sliding down the length of the wire, or falling off before I could connect.

Hours passed. My arm cramped and quivered. Sweat from my hand trickled down the back of my forearm and dripped off the tip of my elbow.

I stopped, took a break and then started to work again, propelled by the thought that Mama would be home soon. I guided the chain up to the lock and heard it miraculously drop back into the notch. The sound of it was almost as sweet as the orange juice.

47

After a lot of practice, I became adept at unlocking and then locking the door to my bedroom. Soon it was routine for me to slip into the kitchen for food at night after everyone else in the family was asleep. It was a good thing too, because school had started back up and this year there were no cafeteria jobs available.

One night, after I had finished my homework, I was hungry for a snack and decided to get something to eat from my stash of food. I went into the short closet, lifted the loose plank, stuck my hand inside the hole and felt around. It was empty. Panic crawled up my spine. *It's gone! My food is all gone! She knows!*

The next morning Mama brought my school clothes to me. "Missing something last night, were you?" She laughed, bending at the waist and slapping her hands on the front of her thighs. "I caught you, again, didn't I, Weasel?" Although she was laughing on the outside, I knew deep down she was pissed off because I had managed to get one over on her.

She found the bent coat hanger in my room and fumed for days trying to figure out how I had used it to unlock the door. In the meantime, she had to come up with other sleeping arrangements for me. I was relocated upstairs to an unfinished attic room, right down the hall from her bedroom. Daddy moved my bed up and I brought the bucket I used to pee in.

My new room had exposed rafters with nails poking through and a rough plywood floor. I didn't like it as much as my room under the stairs because of all the itchy, gray insulation everywhere. But at least it had a window for me to look out.

Mama could watch me more closely up in the attic room; however, she still couldn't sleep easy until she had found a way to keep me from sneaking out and getting into her kitchen again. But she didn't want to scar up any more of the wooden doors with another lock. She fretted over what to do for a few days. Finally Daddy came up with the idea of wedging a two-by-four under my doorknob.

48

It was Monday morning, and my English teacher was handing out our new vocabulary list. She was moving from desk to desk, like she always did, placing a crisp sheet of white paper in front of each student. As she moved up and down the rows of desks, getting closer and closer to mine, I could smell the paper. It was something I'd smelled hundreds of times before, but had never taken notice. Strangely, my mouth began to water, like it did at the sight of Mama's famous fried chicken, and at ten thirty every morning when the school cafeteria started cooking our lunch.

Other than to write on it, I had never paid much attention to paper. No more attention than I'd paid to my number two pencil or blue binder. But when the teacher got to my desk and put my vocabulary list in front of me, I felt an odd urge to grab it, tear off a strip and eat it, like you'd pull off a piece of cotton candy and pop it into your mouth, as soon as the vendor hands it to you.

Lifting the paper to my face, I inhaled. It smelled fresh, like peppermint and the cucumbers from Grandma Storm's garden. I told myself I was just extra hungry, that it wasn't the paper I wanted to eat; I just wanted to eat *something*. I hadn't had breakfast that morning. Not much supper the night before either. I shook the thought from my head and began scanning the vocabulary list.

I couldn't concentrate. The smell of the paper kept calling me, daring me to take a taste. *What would a nibble hurt?* I glanced around the room to see if anybody was watching and of all people, Patty Hostetler, the class know-it-all and the class tattletale, who sat in the desk directly across from me, was staring straight at me, through narrowed eyes. She knew I was up to something.

The teacher called for everyone's attention to go over the new vocabulary words and Patty turned toward the front. While her eyes and everyone else's were occupied, I dog-eared an upper corner of my paper, tore it off at the crease and slipped it between my lips.

The flavor of the paper was even better than the smell, sweet and starchy and chewing it satisfied an unnameable craving from deep inside me. I chewed and chewed until it had dissolved to a mush in my mouth.

As soon as I had swallowed it, I wanted another piece. I looked down at my vocabulary paper with its one missing corner and decided it was lopsided and would probably look better if both top corners matched. After I had eaten the second corner, it occurred to me that the paper now appeared even more off balance than before and it would be best if all four corners matched. So I tore them off and ate them too.

As I was finishing off the last corner, I noticed Patty Hostetler was staring at me again. "You chewing gum?" she whispered.

I swallowed. "No, I'm not chewing gum."

"Are too. I'm telling the teacher, unless you give me a piece."

She started to raise her hand and I stopped her. "Wait a minute! I'm not chewing gum," I whispered. "I'm chewing paper."

"You makin' paper wads? Are you fixin' to spit a paper wad at somebody?" She half-raised her hand again. "I'm tellin'!'"

"I'm not making paper wads!" I said. "Look." I waved my hands in front of me. "I don't even have a straw."

"You just chewin' on paper?"

"Yeah, I'm chewing paper."

"What for?"

"Something to do, I guess."

"You're *weird*."

"Well, maybe I am, but at least I don't have a booger hanging out of my nose!"

She didn't really have a booger on her nose, but it was all I could think of to get her mind off what I was doing.

She clamped one hand over her face and gasped and then groped around in her purse with the other.

The teacher tapped her ink pen on her desk. "I want everyone's attention now! Patty Hostetler, put your purse away and read the definition of word number four to the class."

As Patty read, strip by strip, I shredded and ate the edges of my vocabulary list, until nothing was left of it but the text. When I had eaten all I could without sacrificing the part I had to study for a test, I held what remained of the ragged paper in my hand and became alarmed by how small it had become, by how much of it I had consumed.

We finished going over all the words and I folded what was left of the paper and slipped it into the back of my spiral notebook to take home and study. I shrugged the incident off as no big deal. After all, Marty Travis, a kid in my fourth period, picked his scabs and ate them all the time. And lots of people I knew ate their fingernails. So what if I ate some paper?

Later, alone in my room, the craving came back and I ate three sheets of notebook paper without stopping. When I had finished, I realized I wasn't just nibbling anymore. While I was munching on my vocabulary list earlier in the day, it didn't seem like I was doing anything out of the ordinary. But now I had eaten a substantial amount of something that could make me sick, possibly kill me.

After some tossing about in my bed and worrying over whether or not I was going to die, I fell to sleep, not sure if I would wake up in the morning, but with a full feeling in my belly.

49

Even though my knowledge of right and wrong told me I shouldn't be eating paper, that it was most likely bad for my health, my craving for it, which was much more dominant than my good sense, always won out. I knew what I was doing was not normal. But then, there was nothing about my life that was normal.

Hiding my paper eating was easy; I was good at keeping secrets. But the whole idea that I had suddenly turned into a goat messed with my head. To keep from feeling like a total freak, I told myself that hunger had driven me to such drastic measures and it wasn't my fault. I blamed it on Mama. It was her fault for not feeding me enough.

On the nights when she sent me to bed with no supper and hunger kicked me in the gut, if I had notebook paper in my school binder, I ate it and went to sleep satiated.

After a while I got to where I preferred paper to food. It filled my belly in the same way and quelled a craving that food could not. As I chewed, it often took on the taste of the foods I longed to eat. I could pop a piece of notebook paper into my mouth, close my eyes and think of a huge slice of pizza, or a plate overflowing with spaghetti smothered with meat sauce and the paper would take on the taste I was imagining.

Once I had accepted my bizarre new habit, I turned my attention to finding ways to feed it. Mama allotted me several sheets of notebook paper at the beginning of each week for school, but they didn't last long. Usually I had them eaten by Wednesday night. I was then forced to borrow paper from the kids in my class just so I could do my homework. But sometimes I ate it on the bus before I got home.

Soon my classmates grew tired of lending me notebook paper, forcing me to use most of what Mama gave me for my homework, because I was running out of excuses to give my teachers. With supply limited and my appetite growing, I had to start looking to find other sources to feed my hunger.

I decided to experiment. I thought construction paper would taste good because it was colorful. But I found the dye in it to be too bitter and the spongy texture was not to my liking either. I ate up all my old test papers and work sheets, and the borders of the pages in my school textbooks, until they were craggy, and nothing was left but the words. Sometimes I ripped out random sheets from sections we had already covered—text, pictures and all. But again, I didn't like the taste of the ink and because we had to turn our books back in at the end of the school year, it was not worth the risk of getting caught.

While I was using the restroom at school, pulling the toilet paper from the roll and wrapping it around my hand, it crossed my mind to try a piece. I tore off one perforated section and nibbled at the corner. To my delight, it was delicious, even better than notebook paper. Without any ink, dye, or glue, it tasted pure and it had more of the woody, almost nut-like flavor I had grown to love. While sitting on the toilet, I stuffed the rest of the section into my mouth, followed by another and another, until I had eaten the rest of the roll.

I could barely contain my pride for having discovered a new, better kind of paper to eat. Knowing there was toilet paper inside every stall of the restroom excited me. It was there for my taking and the best part of all was there was an unlimited supply that wouldn't be missed.

In the coming days, I asked to be excused from my classes frequently to use the restroom. I told my teachers I had a bladder infection that made me feel like I always had to go and they bought it. Once I was in the restroom, I locked myself in a stall, tore off the toilet paper, piece by perforated piece, rolled it into a ball and then popped it into my mouth.

Every day after school was dismissed, I went into the restroom and stole whole rolls and stuffed them into my book satchel to take home. I took the paper towels too, the thick, brown kind that also had a nutty flavor I enjoyed.

Now that I was eating large amounts of paper on a daily basis and suffering no side effects, aside from a touch of constipation, it was clear to me that I was not going to die from it. So in my mind I had no reason to stop.

GREYHOUND to A NEW LIFE

5O

I was sitting on the floor of my bedroom with my back pressed against the door. Images of Mama's frightened face as I was twisting her arm kept popping into my head. Suddenly I felt sick to my stomach. I crawled on my hands and knees to my bucket, hung my head over it and gagged, producing only foamy, bitter bile.

After heaving until my ribs caved, I dragged myself to bed, climbed in and collapsed, face down. That's when the tears came. Hurting her was wrong, evil. I knew this, but at the same time it had felt right, just and I hated myself for not having stood up to her sooner. I lay in bed for hours, the two emotions clashing around like crazy in my head, until I fell to sleep, exhausted from dry heaving and crying and thinking.

The sound of my bedroom doorknob rattling woke me. My thoughts were fuzzy for a few seconds while I tried to register what was going on: *Why had the two-by-four not fallen to the floor this time?*

In those few seconds before cognizance, my mind was able to trick itself into believing that what had happened between Mama and me had all been a bad dream.

It could have been. I'd had similar dreams before, graphic ones, in which I had attacked her, beating her like she beat me. Over the years, in my sleep, I had hurt her a hundred times, in a hundred different ways. Sometimes after such a dream, I awoke with some of my rage relieved. What I felt now, lost in a fog of confusion, was an emotion I couldn't identify.

The door opened and there stood Daddy, holding a plate of food in his hand. "I brought you something to eat," he said. "You must be starving; you haven't had anything all day."

"I'm not hungry."

"Well, I'll leave it anyway, in case you change your mind." He sat the plate on the foot of my bed. "Your mama told me what happened earlier today while I was gone."

"I lost my temper," I said. "I didn't mean to hurt her."

"I know you didn't. But I'm surprised it hadn't happened sooner," he said. "You must have done something to scare her, because she doesn't want to get around you anymore."

"I just squeezed her arm...and twisted it a little."

"It doesn't matter. I understand, Tuesday, but you and your mama probably shouldn't live together anymore. I'm going to make arrangements with Macy for you to stay with her in Nashville."

I perked up. "Am I going to school there?"

"You're going to have to finish out this year here—you only have a couple of weeks left—but then you can start ninth grade in Nashville. You're old enough now to stay by yourself after school while Macy's at work."

He turned and left the room. Right before he closed the door behind him, he said, "Try to eat something."

I heard him put the two-by-four back under the doorknob.

51

Two weeks later, on Saturday, I got up early to catch an 8:00 a.m. Greyhound to Nashville. That morning I walked about my room like a robot, collecting my things, as if I had been programmed to move forward, do what needed to be done, without thinking, without feeling.

It didn't take me long to pack. Everything I owned fit tightly into one of Daddy's old duffle bags. He carried it out to the car for me, while I stayed behind and took one final look around my room to make sure I had gotten everything.

Before I went downstairs, I walked down the hallway to Mama's bedroom, and stood in the doorway watching her sleep. She was lying on her back with one of her arms stretched up over her head. The sheet was draped over one shoulder and wrapped around the curves of her body. A placid expression was on her face. She reminded me of a statue of a Greek goddess like one I had seen when Grandma Storm had taken me to the Parthenon in Nashville.

Standing there, it occurred to me she hadn't even bothered to get up and see me off before I left home for good. *Don't you have any love for me left in your heart? Have you forgotten the day*

I was born? When I said my first words, took my first steps? Have I done anything in the last five years that touched you, made you proud?

I turned away from her and walked down the stairs to the front door.

"Did you get everything?" Daddy asked when I got outside.

He waited for my nod and then we got in the car.

We backed out of the drive and I watched the house as it got farther and farther away. I knew I would not miss the place the way I had missed our house on Maplewood Drive after we moved to Kentucky. I had made no good memories there. I wouldn't even miss my brothers because they had become strangers to me.

I felt awkward sitting beside this man I'd come to hardly know at all. When we got on the road, I turned my face to the window and watched the trees and telephone poles pass by.

After about ten minutes passed, Daddy cleared his throat. "It's finally over, Tuesday, over for you, at least."

I understood what he meant. He couldn't have been at peace with Mama's constant accusations and violent fits, which had gotten progressively worse over the years. Now that I was leaving, the focus of her anger would be solely on him.

"You don't have to take it, Daddy. You can leave too, you know."

"I can't leave your mama. She wouldn't be able to take care of herself or properly look after the boys; she can't even write a check on her own."

"Whatever you say, Daddy," I said. I hoped my sarcasm came through.

He didn't have a comeback and I couldn't think of anything else to say, so I turned and looked out the window again. We needed to talk about so much, but neither of us knew where to begin. During that thirty-minute drive to the Greyhound Bus station in a neighboring town, there were many unanswered questions lost in the void of silence between us.

Daddy pulled into the parking lot of the bus station and turned off the car engine. He sat there for a minute, staring straight ahead, his knuckles white on the steering wheel. Then he turned to me. "Sweetheart, I'm sorry things were not always easy for you. I can't take it all back; it's too late for that. But at least I know you will be happy now."

I tried to think of something to say to him in response, a terse, profound statement that would haunt him for the rest of his life. But I couldn't. And even if I could have found the right words, I wouldn't have been able to get them past the lump that was swelling in my throat. All I could manage was a slight smile.

He unloaded my duffle bag of clothes from the car and I followed him into the bus station. "Macy will pick you up when you get to Nashville," he said. "It should be around eleven o'clock this morning." He glanced at his watch. "I've got to go now. Mama and the boys will be up soon. I'll call you in a few days."

We hugged, touching only our shoulders and then he left the bus station. Right before he got to the door, he stopped, reached into the back pocket of his pants and pulled something out. "Here, I almost forgot," he said, extending an envelope to me. "Take this; it's your ticket, and some spending money. There's a note from your mama in there too."

As he loped across the parking lot, taking long, purposeful strides, my heart lurched toward him. So many times I had seen him walk away like that when he dropped me off at

Grandma's for the summer. I was always sad then, because I knew he wouldn't be back until school started. Now, as he left, I wondered when I would see him again. I watched him until a bus pulled up in front of the station and blocked him from my view.

According to the clock behind the counter, I still had about ten minutes before my bus left. I sat on a bench, opened the envelope Daddy had given me and pulled out the contents: a one-way bus ticket to Nashville, four twenty-dollar bills and a folded piece of notebook paper with nothing written on the outside. I crumpled the letter into a wad and tossed it into a nearby trash can.

The lady behind the ticket counter announced over the loudspeaker that the bus for Nashville was now boarding. I got my things together and joined the flow of people walking out the door. Suddenly, right before I boarded the bus, I had a change of heart and went back into the station and retrieved Mama's letter from the trashcan and stuffed it into the front pocket of my jeans.

52

Aunt Macy was happy to see me when she picked me up at the bus station in Nashville. She acted like she always had when I'd spent my summers with her and Grandma Storm.

She didn't want to talk much about why I was coming to live with her. In the car, on the way to her house, I told her Mama had done some mean things to me and she said she'd suspected I wasn't treated like the boys but she never knew how bad it was. She didn't want to hear the details, though. Avoiding uncomfortable situations seemed to run in the family.

"I lost my temper when Mama was kicking me and I grabbed her arm and twisted it," I said. "I didn't mean to, Aunt Macy, I was just so mad."

"Well, honey, you know what they say, you can only beat a dog so much before he turns on you."

That summer, I was content to hang around Aunt Macy's house and to do what most people take for granted. I lounged on the sofa watching television for hours and ate all the foods I never got at home: hamburgers, pizza and chocolate chip cookies, right from the oven. At night I delighted in soaking in a bubble bath and then climbing into bed between crisp, clean sheets.

Aunt Macy let me do pretty much anything I pleased that summer. She did get a little aggravated with me for hoarding food in my room, though. She found open bags of potato chips and snack cakes under my bed and unwrapped cookies nestled between the clothes in my drawers.

"All that food lying around is going to draw mice," she said.

I knew she was right but, for a while, I just couldn't shake the feeling that I might need the food someday, that somehow I would be left with nothing to eat.

When school started, everything changed. Aunt Macy made sure I had all the supplies I needed and plenty of nice clothes to wear. But I soon found out it was going to take a lot more than new clothes to transform me into a normal kid.

While I had lived at home, my struggle to survive had defined me. It had given me a reason to be miserable, to be bitter. It had provided me with a convenient excuse for not fitting in or excelling in school. It was why I didn't have any friends. Without it as my driving force, I had no idea who I was, or what to do with myself. All at once, I had decisions to make, choices before me.

The kids in Nashville were different from the ones in Uniontown, where everybody knew everybody and popularity was synonymous with money. There were too many people in Nashville for them all to know one another, and whether or not your parents were rich didn't seem to be nearly as important. But just because I had been granted the freedom to pursue a social life didn't mean I knew how to have one. After what happened with Kat, I had become withdrawn and gotten into the habit of creating a distance between myself and other people, if not a wall.

Interacting at school was difficult. I didn't know how to go about starting a conversation with someone. So, just to have something interesting to talk about, I decided to tell a few people about some of the things Mama had done to me.

When I heard myself talking to someone about how bad my life used to be, it sounded surreal. Although I knew everything I was saying was true, it seemed more like I was describing a bizarre dream, or a tragic movie I'd seen. After I had finished, they glared at me with an incredulous expression, probably stunned both by the horrific nature of my story and the emotionless, detached way I was able to tell it.

Nobody came right out and said I was lying, but I could often see the doubt in their eyes. They were kids raised in healthy, nurturing environments and they simply could not process the notion of a mother turning vicious against her own child. They had been taught that by virtue of nature a mother always accepts her offspring and that God—the same God who holds the mother sacred and tells us to honor and love her unconditionally—would never allow for such evil.

When people didn't believe me, or didn't believe it had been as bad as what I said, I wasn't offended. I got it. I preferred their disbelief to the alternative reaction, which was pity. When I saw sympathy dawn in someone's eyes, I tried to reassure them, and maybe myself, with the tone of my voice that I had come through it okay. But I knew I hadn't, not completely. I was aware of the emptiness within, a gaping hole inside, where it felt like something of substance should have been.

The next time I saw the people I had told about my life at home, I noticed they were standoffish, as if they no longer knew how to act around me, what to say. Or they were afraid my abusive childhood had left me too emotionally disturbed to get involved with. This made me realize that what had happened to me separated me from the normal world in a negative way. Like a handicap or a disfiguring deformity, it was too horrible for some people to deal with and it made them uncomfortable whenever they were around me.

Since normal was what I was shooting for, what I had always been shooting for, I decided it would be best to stop talking about my past altogether, to extract it from my future like a dentist extracts an abscessed tooth. I thought if I could stop it from poisoning me, I would fit in with the other kids and could then attempt something that at least resembled normal.

Whenever I met someone for the first time, it was my chance to, in a sense, begin again with people not influenced by the knowledge of what I'd been through. Each friend I made was another piece in the puzzle of my new life. While I was able to push my old, damaged life away, I soon became good at feigning normalcy enough to fit in at school. But just because I had stopped talking about the past didn't mean it wasn't still there, working its way to the surface.

In my mind's eye, I can see Mama sitting in front of her vanity putting on her makeup. She is trying out shade after shade of lipstick and eye shadow, wiping her face clean in between applications, the crumpled wads of pink tissue piling high in the wastebasket beside her. One minute she has tweezers in her hand and is plucking at her eyebrows; the next, she's picking at the bumps on her face. Her hair is up; her hair is down. After hours of this, she switches off the rose-colored lamp on her vanity, draws the thickly lined draperies that make her bedroom dark and safe and climbs back into bed for the rest of the day.

All of Mama's emphasis on my looks had planted a seed deep within my subconscious that was one day destined to sprout. Now that I was in control of my appearance, it became my life mission to be beautiful like she had been at my age.

My insecurities, like hers, compelled me to spend too much time in front of my own mirror trying to improve the image I saw by changing my makeup and experimenting with different hairstyles, not sure what I was striving for. I got up at four in the morning because it took me at least three hours to get ready for the day. Everything, my makeup, my hair, my clothes had to be perfect before I faced a single person. By a single person, I mean the mail carrier, the trash collector, the three-year-old girl who lived next door—anyone.

I discovered that, in a way, I had been comfortable hiding behind my plainness, and that being attractive was much more difficult and stressful than being ugly, because it brought with it pressure to remain that way.

Aunt Macy told me I would be a better, happier person if I didn't allow myself to worry so much about superficial matters and that I should try to develop a more enduring sense of self-worth. I tried to take her advice, and with the help of her positive reinforcement, most days I was okay with my appearance. Still, there were other times when I'd look in the mirror, or the murky glass of a car window, and catch a glimpse of the hollow cheeks and elongated jaw line of the homely girl Mama had once called horse face.

53

If my theory of why I had started eating paper in the first place was true I should have had no reason to do it while I was living with Aunt Macy. No reason to wake in the middle of the night, like before, with the familiar craving.

But one night I did.

I tried to shake it off and go back to sleep, but I couldn't. I got up and went into the kitchen and ate whatever food I could get my hands on the quickest: a cookie, a few bites of ice cream and a handful of peanuts. But none of it satisfied my hunger, because I wasn't hungry for food.

On my way back to bed, I stopped at the bathroom to pee. When I'd finished, I tore off a length of toilet paper from the roll and wrapped it around my hand, like I usually did, preparing to wipe myself. But before the paper made it to its destination, it somehow found its way into my mouth.

It was the thick, soft kind with a perfume scent and I didn't especially like the flavor of it, or the texture, nearly as much as I did the school toilet paper. But I didn't hate it either. It was better than nothing, and enough to silence my intense craving.

As had become my ritual, I pulled off section after section, rolled it into a ball and then popped it into my mouth. Not until I had reached the cardboard center did I realize I had eaten the entire roll of paper and had not yet wiped myself. There I was, stranded on the toilet, searching around me for something to wipe with. Finally, I found a box of Kleenex on the tank behind me.

Ashamed and confused, I went back to bed. I could have had anything I wanted to eat from Macy's well-stocked kitchen and I still wanted toilet paper. My strange compulsion could no longer be blamed on hunger. I had to face up to the obvious truth: I was a bona fide freak.

The next day I was in full force with my paper eating again. By the end of the week, I had gone through two more rolls of toilet paper and one roll of paper towels.

"Tuesday, do you have any idea what happened to the package of toilet paper I bought at the grocery store yesterday?" Aunt Macy asked, one afternoon when I got in from school.

"I guess maybe I could be using too much to wipe," I said. "I'll try to do better."

"You have no reason to lie to me," Aunt Macy said, squaring her eyes up with mine. "Whatever you need the paper for, I'm sure I'll understand."

No you wouldn't. "I didn't take it, Aunt Macy, I promise!"

She took me by the back of one of my arms and led me to my bedroom. She then went to all my hiding places—under my bed, in my sock drawer, and on the top shelf of my closet behind my sweaters—and pulled out a roll of toilet paper from each one. She piled them in the center of my bed. "Now, what is all this paper doing in your room?"

I still couldn't bring myself to tell her. "I don't know!" I said, now crying.

She gathered the toilet paper up into her arms and started walking toward my bedroom door. Before she left the room, she turned around. "You think about this, Tuesday, and when you're ready to tell me the truth, I'll be in the living room waiting to talk."

Even after I had calmed down, I still wasn't ready to tell Aunt Macy I ate paper. I didn't know how to tell her. I was afraid saying the words out loud would make it too real. I got into bed, pulled the covers up over my face and lay there until I fell asleep.

I woke up in the middle of the night, thirsty, and went into the kitchen to get a glass of milk. Before I went back to bed, I stopped to use the bathroom. When I'd finished peeing, I pulled some toilet paper from the roll, wiped myself and then got up and left the room, turning the light out behind me.

Right outside the door, I stopped, and then went back in. I put down the lid of the toilet, sat on top of it, and then kicked the door shut. In the dark, I unrolled a length of toilet paper about two feet long and ate it, one sheet at a time. Some of the sheets I placed on my tongue, allowing them to dissolve slowly. Others I rolled into a ball and chewed to a pulp.

Just as I'd placed the last sheet into my mouth, all of a sudden the bathroom door swung open, and I was blinded by the overhead light. Aunt Macy was standing in the doorway looking straight at me. Sitting there, with a piece of toilet paper hanging from my mouth, a strange sense of calm and relief that someone finally knew washed over me.

"Tuesday Leigh Storm, what are you doing?" she asked, taking a step toward me to get a better view. "Is that toilet paper? Why do you have toilet paper in your mouth?" She stomped the rest of the way over to me and thrust her hand under my chin. "Spit it out! Spit it out this instant! It'll make you sick!"

"It won't make me sick," I said. "I've done it before."

"You have? When?"

"Lots of times."

"Tuesday, spit that paper in the toilet and come into the kitchen with me. I'll make you some hot chocolate."

We talked for two hours that night. I told her everything: when I started eating paper, what had made me want to try it in the first place, how often I ate it and how much. She listened to every word I had to say without calling me a freak or running from the room, mortified.

I explained to her that sometimes Mama didn't give me enough food and that I thought I had started eating paper because I was hungry.

"If that's the case, then why are you still eating it?" she asked. "Are you getting enough food now?"

"Yes, I am, and that's why I can't figure out why I'm still doing it. I've tried to stop, Aunt Macy, I have, but I can't, the urge is too strong."

"Well, I think the first thing we need to do is get you to a doctor to see if eating paper has done any damage to your digestive system. It's a wonder you're not stopped up tighter than a drum. And while we're there, I'll ask him if he knows *why* you would be craving such a thing in the first place. There has to be a reason. There is a reason for everything."

54

I was sitting on the corner of an examination table waiting for the doctor to come in. Aunt Macy was across the room from me in a short chair with wheels. I squirmed around, shifting from butt cheek to butt cheek, crinkling and tearing the paper beneath me.

"Sit still, Tuesday," said Aunt Macy. "You're making *me* nervous!"

"What am I going to say to the doctor?" I asked.

"You're going to tell him the same thing you told me."

"I can't just tell some stranger I eat paper."

"Yes, you can. You have to."

"No, no, Aunt Macy, please don't make me say it!"

"Well, I'll tell him then."

"Okay. How will you tell him?"

"I don't know," she said, fidgeting with the straps of her purse. "I'll think of something when the time comes."

"Pretend he's in here, right now. What would you say?"

"I don't know."

"Come on, Aunt Macy, this is about me! I need to know what you're going to say to him."

"Well, I'd probably say something like, 'Dr. Jernigan, Tuesday here has a problem we need to talk to you about.'"

Just then the doorknob turned, and in walked a short, stocky man with salt and pepper hair. Like the doctors I'd seen on television, he was wearing a white lab jacket and holding a clipboard. He closed the door behind him. There was no escape.

"Hi, Macy, good to see you again," he said.

Aunt Macy extended her hand to him, and he squeezed it. "Good morning, Dr. Jernigan."

He turned to me. "And who do we have here?"

"This is my niece, Tuesday," Aunt Macy said. "Actually, she's the reason we came in to visit you today."

"Hi, Tuesday! What a lovely name."

"Thanks. I was named after the actress, Tuesday Weld."

"Is that so? Well what brings you to my office today Miss named-after-a-movie-star, Tuesday?"

I looked at Aunt Macy.

"Well, it's kind of unusual, Dr. Jernigan. You see, Tuesday feels fine, and I believe she's perfectly healthy, but she's developed this strange habit." She paused, and my heart did somersaults. "She eats paper."

And just like that, my hideous secret was out in the open and all of a sudden, I was sitting there naked in front of a man I had just met.

Dr. Jernigan turned to me. "That certainly *is* an unusual habit," he said.

Inspecting my feet, I cringed in preparation for his laughter. Or for him to get up and rush out of the office, saying something like, "I'm sorry, but I can't help you, I'll have to send you to a specialist."

But he didn't do either one.

"Tuesday, you probably thought I would think you were a freak when I heard about this, but I don't," he said. "And I'm pretty sure I know why you do it too."

My ears pricked. "You do?"

"Yes, I believe I do. Of course, I'll have to run a few tests to make sure and to rule out some other possibilities, but I feel strongly about my suspicions."

"Well, what do you think it is, Dr. Jernigan?" Aunt Macy asked. "Is it something serious?"

"It's called pica and the disorder itself is not serious. But the reason why she has pica and the result of eating paper could be, if we allow it to go on for too long." He pulled another chair in front of me and sat in it. "Truth be told, you're a lucky young lady, Tuesday, because another physician might not have picked up on it. If I hadn't had a personal experience with pica, chances are I wouldn't have either. You see, a few years back, when my baby sister was pregnant with her first child, she started craving non-food items."

"She ate paper too?" I asked.

"No, I believe her tastes leaned more toward chalk. And, I think drywall."

"Really?" I was giddy to find out there was another person on earth who ate things besides food. Even though it was chalk that she ate instead of paper, which in my mind was even stranger, knowing about it made me feel a lot less freakish. Realizing I'd sounded a bit too excited about his sister's misfortune, I tried to talk more serious. "What made her want to eat chalk?"

"She had an iron deficiency caused by her pregnancy."

"But I'm not pregnant," I said.

He chuckled. "I know you're not, but there could be another reason why the iron in your blood might be low. Have you started your period yet?"

I put my head down in shame. "No."

Aunt Macy came to my rescue. "The women in our family are all late bloomers; I didn't start until I was almost sixteen. Tuesday is about to turn fifteen."

"The reason I ask is because women lose a lot of iron through their monthly menstrual flow and sometimes this makes them anemic. But if you haven't started yet, I don't know what else could be making a healthy young lady like you low on iron." He lifted one of his eyebrows. "You haven't been dieting, have you?"

"Oh, no," I said without having to think about it. "I eat like a pig!"

Aunt Macy backed me up. "She's telling the truth. You wouldn't know it to look at her, but this girl eats everything in sight." She glanced over at me. "Sorry, Tuesday, I didn't mean it the way it sounded."

"Hmmm, now that *is* unusual," the doctor said. "But I promise we'll get to the bottom of it. I'll definitely have to run some tests before I know anything for sure." He got up from his seat and moved toward the door. "I'll have a nurse come in and draw blood right away."

After the nurse had taken my blood, Dr. Jernigan came back in the examination room and talked to us some more. He said that when his sister experienced pica, he did some research on it. He found out it was more common than he thought and that there were people all over the world who ate not only chalk and paper, but everything from dirt to cigarette ashes. The more he talked the more normal I became.

"What is her name, your sister?" I asked him, longing to put an identity to, and make human this woman who had saved me.

"Pamela Sue—we call her Pam for short."

"Is she pretty?"

"Pretty doesn't do her justice. She was homecoming queen in high school."

Like Mama! I thought. "Wow!" I said. "Does she still eat chalk?"

"No, but she says she still wants to sometimes, and you probably will want to eat paper for a while too, even after we get your iron level up. Most pica patients say eating non-food items becomes an addiction, a way to relieve anxiety. When your test results come back, if indeed your iron is low, I'll start you on supplements right away, and that should help."

A few days later, Dr. Jernigan called with the results of my blood test. As he had suspected, my iron level was low. He wrote a prescription for supplements, and Aunt Macy and I went to the drugstore that afternoon to get it filled. I took one of the pills in the car before we got home.

"Now, Tuesday, remember Dr. Jernigan said that the iron supplements won't work right away," she reminded me.

"I know, but it won't hurt to get started."

She laughed. It sounded like a laugh of relief.

55

After I moved out, Daddy called me at Aunt Macy's at least once a week, but to keep peace at home, he didn't tell Mama.

Our conversations were usually short. Mostly we talked about what I was doing in school. Each time before we hung up, he stalled, acting as if he wanted to say something more, but didn't know how. There were things I wanted to discuss with him too, but I never could summons the guts. Afterward, I was always left disappointed that we never broke the surface of what really needed to be said. Our inability to talk about the past was almost as damaging to our relationship as the past itself.

My frustrations with our phone conversations led me to believe the effort to have a relationship with him wasn't worth it, that I would be happier if I cut off all contact with him. For a while, I refused his phone calls. I even went so far as to throw away everything I had that reminded me of him— birthday cards he'd sent and pictures of himself he'd given to me. I thought if I no longer had these traces of him in my sight it would be easier to let him go from my life.

But then they would come back to me, the sweet mornings of my early childhood when I lay in my bed listening to him singing in the kitchen as he made breakfast. The times he came to my room to tell me he loved me, with an obscure sadness in his eyes. How each passing day, he grew more despondent and more consumed with guilt for what he was allowing to happen, his gaze dropping lower and lower each time I saw him, until he could no longer make eye contact with me. When I thought of this, I always went weak for him again and later found myself digging in the wastebasket for the mementoes I had thrown away.

From an early age, because of my love for him, my view of the significant part he played in my unhappy life at home was distorted. It was my heart that defended his actions for all those years, persuading me that his weakness was only where Mama was concerned and his devotion to her was what crippled him. He appeared strong to the public world, his very presence commanding respect from everyone around him. But at home, behind closed doors, he was forced to let down his façade and be dominated by a disturbed woman. This overwhelming pity I felt, coupled with my empathy for him for having been another one of Mama's victims, always managed to suppress any resentment I harbored.

As I grew older, my mind sometimes told me to blame him for everything, to make him pay for not helping me, but my heart wanted nothing more than to curl up in his lap and hear him say he loved me.

Now, a teenager, I'd grown to hate his passiveness, his need to escape confrontation and turn away from the uncomfortable issues in his life. While I hated these traits, which to me defined him, defined his character, and while I had lost some of the respect I'd once had for him as a man, I could never bring myself to hate *him*. He was still, and would always be, my daddy.

"Hold on a little longer," he had said when I was eight. In some ways I was still holding on, waiting for him to come through. I wanted to believe that one day he would keep his promise and make everything right.

On a Sunday morning, after church, Daddy came to Aunt Macy's for a visit. When he arrived, we embraced. It was good to have him hold me again, but I could still feel something unyielding wedged between us, something with the rigidity of a thick wall.

Aunt Macy prepared tuna sandwiches and potato salad for lunch. She toasted and buttered the bread of the sandwiches, and made the potato salad from real mashed potatoes. While we ate, we were able to laugh and engage in light-hearted conversation. After lunch Aunt Macy offered to clean up the kitchen, so Daddy and I could take our iced teas out onto the front porch and talk.

As soon as we got outside, he brought up the forbidden subject. "I want to say some things to you about what happened with you and your mama." He raked his fingers through his hair. It was a familiar gesture, something he had always done when he was nervous. "You know she was never right after her accident," he said. "When she started acting strange with you, I assumed it was because of the brain injury and that she would get better, like the doctor said. I kept hoping it would all stop."

"But even if her brain injury caused her to mistreat me, it still wasn't right."

"No, of course it wasn't, honey. That's not what I'm saying." He drained his glass of tea. "After the first time she went too far, I thought—hoped—it was an isolated incident. We had an argument over it. Then there was another incident and another argument."

I understood what he meant, how things got out of hand quickly. Every day she continued to test her limits with him. The more she got by with, the more empowered she became, until after a while it was evident to her that neither he, nor anyone else was going to stop her.

"I know you tried in the beginning," I said. "I haven't forgotten the times you went to battle for me."

"When she wouldn't stop, I considered leaving. God knows I love that woman with every fiber of my being, and still I thought I should divorce her for what she was doing to you, even though I knew in my heart she was sick. But I was afraid to, afraid she would get custody of all of you kids—the woman usually does, you know—and then there would have been nothing I could have done to make your life better. Bottom line is, after I let it go too far I didn't know how to fix the problem. All I knew to do was get you away from her as much as possible. That's why I took you to your Grandma Storm's every summer."

He was trying to convince me—and himself—of what he was saying, that he had taken his only recourse, been forced into his decisions. But his eyes revealed that he still carried the burden of his guilt and had not been able to forgive himself.

"I'm thankful you at least did that, Daddy."

"Tuesday, I want you to know I was wrong. I should have done more. I don't know what I should have done, but I should have done something. I guess I didn't want to face how bad the situation had become." He raked his fingers through his hair again. "I am so, so, sorry."

I could have left it at that, given him a second chance, started all over with a blank canvas. And I felt like I was right on the verge of following through, but my pain and anger got in the way and I ended up lashing out at him instead.

"I can forgive you for not doing anything early on," I said. "But when the social worker came to the house, you had the perfect opportunity to help me and you didn't."

"Come on, Tuesday, do you really think the social worker would have simply whisked you off to a loving home somewhere? Believe me, that's not the way things would have played out. It would have been difficult to prove what happened to you." The way he put it made it sound as if I had been the victim of some unfortunate accident that he'd had nothing to do with. "You know your mama can be pretty persuasive. She would have made it hard for me to convince the social worker she was capable of such cruelty. And even if I did, at that point, how would I have explained why I had allowed it to go on for so long? What if we both had been deemed unfit parents? They might have taken you and the boys away from us and placed you all in different foster homes. Our family could have been ripped apart."

I hadn't thought of that. He was right; no matter what he did the ending was sure to be ugly. "So there was nothing you could have done to help me without hurting everyone else in the family."

"Maybe it was the wrong decision, but at the time, it seemed like the only thing to do."

There was a short stretch of silence. "I wish you could have known the person I fell in love with," he said, his face softening with affection at the mere thought of Mama.

He fell in love with the beautiful and strong young woman who once took care of a sick daughter all by herself. He believed there was good in her because he'd once seen it. He kept hoping she would get better and he wouldn't have to give her up. He loved me too, but not nearly as much as he loved Mama and when it came to the ultimate sacrifice, he couldn't come through for me. His fear of losing her was too great.

"I *did* know that person!" I shouted. "I loved her too! But she went away and the one who replaced her was horrible to me!"

"The bump on her head is what changed her. Something was knocked loose in that fall. She never mistreated you before she fell down those stairs. It wasn't until after her accident that she got the notion that somehow it was your fault Audrey was dead and there was no convincing her otherwise.

"So she *does* think I gave Audrey the flu?"

"Yes, but she had her suspicions of that before she fell down the stairs and she didn't blame you for it then. We discussed it, and she realized you weren't the only one in the house with the flu. Any one of us could have given it to Audrey. For the life of me, I can't figure out why she turned on you and singled you out to blame.

"I know why."

"Why?"

"Because I *am* to blame."

"Oh, honey, that's ridiculous!"

"Does Mama know about the bubble-gum? Did Audrey tell her before she died?"

"Bubble-gum? Rose never mentioned anything about bubble-gum. What on earth are you talking about?"

"I let Audrey chew on some bubble-gum from my mouth the night before I woke up with the flu. I'm the one who caused her to get sick."

"Maybe you *were* the one who gave her the flu. Or maybe it was me. I got sick the same time you did. Remember? And

I kissed Audrey that night before I went to bed." He got up, walked over to where I was sitting and knelt down in front of me. "Tuesday, I can't believe you have carried this with you all of these years." He put his arms around me. "It wasn't your fault Audrey died. If it hadn't been the Hong Kong flu that killed her, it would have been something else. Audrey was a very sick girl, and she had already lived much longer than she was expected to."

"But there's more, Daddy. I *wanted* Audrey to die."

"I'll bet your brothers secretly hoped she would die too. I mean, she did make life harder on all of us and there were so many things we couldn't do as a family because of her. Hell, as much as I loved that kid there were times when I was jealous of her because she took so much of your mama's attention."

"I want to believe you, Daddy, but it would help if I could talk to Mama and find out what she thinks."

"Tuesday, we both know that's a bad idea. It won't get you anywhere to talk to your mama, because she refuses to discuss that part of her life. Somehow she has managed to block out everything she did to you."

"How do you know she won't talk about it?"

"Because I've tried to get her to, many times."

"Well, if she has blocked it all out then why does she think I left home?"

"She thinks you are a troubled teenager. She thinks you had to leave because you tried to hurt her."

"Oh, she remembers that part, huh?"

"All I'm saying is you may have to find a way to deal with what happened to you without talking to your mama about it. If you ever want to try to have a future with her you may have to learn to let go of the past."

"I'm not sure if I know how to do that, Daddy."

"I realize you've suffered, Tuesday, but I think you may have forgotten your mama has suffered too."

"I know. She suffered! She had a crippled daughter who died young! I get it, I do, but that didn't give her the right to take it out on me."

"No, of course not, but it still doesn't change the fact."

Aunt Macy walked out onto the front porch, all smiles. "Anybody up for a game of croquet?" she asked.

Before he left, Daddy went to his car and pulled some sheets of notebook paper from the console. He brought them to me. "I was taking out the trash the other day and I noticed your mama had thrown out a journal she had started right after Audrey died. There aren't many pages; she only wrote in it for a couple of months. I kept some of it for myself, but I brought you a few entries where she had written about you. I thought you might like to have them."

April 7, 1970

My name is Rosalind Marie Storm. I am starting this journal because my husband, Nick, says I should write down my thoughts and feelings, that purging might help me deal with my pain. My Nick is the smartest man I know, so I will give it a try.

I guess I should begin by writing about Audrey, because losing her is the source of my pain. Before she died I had the perfect family, two girls and two boys. Some people may say my family was not perfect because of Audrey, but I say she is the one who made it perfect. She was an angel on earth, and now she is an angel in heaven. She gave me a purpose. Now that she is gone my life feels lopsided. There is a hole where she once was. But I have to go on. I have other children who need me, two wonderful boys, and I still have a daughter, my beautiful Tuesday.

April 12, 1970

I've been thinking, and have come to the conclusion that Tuesday is most likely the one who gave Audrey the flu, but it wasn't her fault she died. My angel had already lived much longer than the doctors told me she would. Tuesday is a smart and sensitive little girl and I am so afraid she will blame herself. I have been watching her closely for signs. So far I think she's okay.

July 11, 1970,

It's Tuesday's birthday! She's eight years old! I bought her a special gift I can't wait to give her. I'm going to fix all her favorite foods, and of course I'll bake her favorite cake, German chocolate. I want to make her day perfect to let her know how much I love her.

For days I read the journal again and again, running my finger over the words "my beautiful Tuesday." I kept thinking about my conversation with Daddy, replaying it in my head and vacillating between throwing the last shovel of dirt over my past and digging up the old bones. Although I had taken comfort in his words, I could not get closure from what he'd told me. I needed to talk to Mama. She had the answers I thought would help me move forward.

A week shy of my fifteenth birthday, I asked Aunt Macy if instead of buying me a present she would drive me to Kentucky to surprise Mama with a visit. She was not enthused with the idea because she, like Daddy, was afraid it might end badly. But after two straight days of my persistent begging, she caved and agreed to take me anyway, against her better judgment.

56

Outside Mama's locked bedroom, I stared at the flickering television light coming from the crack under the door. She had made it clear she did not want to see me, sending word through Daddy that she had a dreadful migraine and would likely be down for the day. But I refused to give up. I kept thinking she'd have come out to go to the bathroom sooner or later.

Two, three, four hours passed—nothing happened. Then I saw her shadow flit across the floor, and a square of folded notebook paper appeared at the bottom of the door. The sight of the note irritated me. I had a sudden urge to wad it up into a tight ball and pop it into my mouth, like a gumdrop and chew it until it was nothing more than a sweet, starchy pulp in my teeth.

But I couldn't. Daddy, who didn't even know I ate paper, was standing right behind me and so was Aunt Macy, to whom I had made a promise that I would make a serious effort to stop. And I hadn't eaten any for almost three months, at least not a substantial amount. Every now and then, I snuck a nosh—a straw wrapper here, a section of toilet paper there— but nothing like before. The craving still remained, although not as strong as it once had been. The doctor had warned me it might, especially during times of stress.

I stooped down, picked up the note and flipped it around to see if my name was written anywhere on the outside. It wasn't. I unfolded it and read, in Mama's familiar backward-slant handwriting, these few words: *I'm feeling under the weather, and wouldn't be good company today. Go home with Aunt Macy and enjoy your birthday.* It was unsigned.

Carefully I refolded the letter, following the creases Mama had created, wondering what she had been thinking as she'd run her fingers across the seams.

"I'm sorry, sweetheart, but she's not ready yet," Daddy said.

Aunt Macy put her arm around me and pulled me in to her. "It's getting late, honey. It's time we go home now."

In the car, I looked out the passenger window as Aunt Macy backed her old Buick out of the drive. I had been so sure about my idea to surprise Mama with a visit, so sure it was the right thing to do, the right time. On the drive up, I had daydreamed about our reunion, envisioning it to be tender and cathartic, culminating with both of us in tears, our arms wrapped around each other, the beginning of a new life together. It never once occurred to me that she might refuse to see me on my birthday. If she would not see me, I had no choice but to walk away. But I knew if I walked away and we had no contact, we may never bond again as mother and daughter and the damage to our relationship and the pain between us would never be resolved.

"Want to stop at Shoney's for supper?" Aunt Macy asked, trying to infuse joy into her voice. "I don't know about you, but I'm starving. And after all, it's your birthday! We should be celebrating!"

Normally the mention of supper at my favorite restaurant would have perked me up. Not this time. "I'm not very hungry," I said. "I just want to go home."

She didn't press. She never did. She always knew what to say, what not to say. I kept my face turned to the window the entire trip. I knew if I looked her I would start to cry.

Back home, in my room, I pulled a dusty shoebox from under my bed and put the note from Mama in it.

As I was placing the lid back on, I noticed a photograph inside, one that Daddy had given me, of Mama and me on my eighth birthday. We were outside on the back patio sitting in her lawn chair. I took the photograph out of the box, turned it over and read what was written on the back: *Ladybug and me.*

I sat on my bed and began removing, one by one, the remaining contents from the box, arranging them in a row in front of me. There were two pictures of Daddy, taken when he was a coach in Spring Hill, crinkled because I had once thrown them away out of anger and confusion. One of Grandma Storm and me that Aunt Macy had taken after church, at Centennial Park in Nashville. I looked so happy in my new yellow pin-dot dress, Grandma holding my hand. I then came across a photo of Audrey and me when she was about fourteen and I was five. I was leaning up against her wheelchair with my arm around her shoulders. Our heads were touching and both of us were smiling. I saw a resemblance I had never noticed before. *I sure could use a sister right about now,* I thought, and stuck the photograph in my mirror where I could see it. There was also a photo of Mama when she was younger, a few years before she'd given birth to me. She was sitting on the front steps of our house on Maplewood Drive, squinting against the sun.

She had on a dark plaid dress that was cinched at the waist. Because the photograph was in black and white, I couldn't tell what color it was, but I imagined it to be coral. It was a color she liked to wear, a color that became her. "She was beautiful," I whispered.

Then I came to the letter from Mama that Daddy had given to me the day I left home. It too was crumpled because I'd thrown it in the trash at the bus station. I had decided to keep it for reasons that were not clear to me then, but I had not yet gathered the courage to read what was written inside. I hoped, as I opened it up, that she had started with "Dear Tuesday." If she had, it would've been the first time she'd acknowledged my name since I was eight. I smoothed out the wrinkles with the palm of my hand and read the single line written inside: *We are always more discontented with others when we are discontented with ourselves.*

Only Mama knew what she had meant by those words when she wrote them. She could have been trying to give me some kind of message about the anger I had shown toward her before I left home. Or maybe she was referring to her own discontent, taking ownership for what she had done and letting me know it wasn't my fault. But if she wouldn't talk to me about our past together I would never find out.

All that remained in the box were napkins from fast-food restaurants, gum wrappers and pieces of wrinkled notebook paper, on which I had written memories from my early childhood. Not long after I left home, things began to surface, thoughts I had kept secluded in a dimly lit corner of my mind, thoughts too ugly to expose in daylight. I wrote what I remembered as it came to me, on any scrap of paper I could find, and then tucked it away in the box. Transferring my anger and pain onto paper turned it into something tangible, something that could be shredded or burned, or at the very least sealed shut in a box.

After I had written down all that I could remember, I stored the box on a shelf in my closet, not sure what I ultimately intended to do with it. Later, when Aunt Macy and I did our annual spring-cleaning, clearing away the accumulated clutter from our closets and drawers, I ran across it. I couldn't bring myself to throw it away, but I wasn't ready to open it either, so I moved it under my bed, out of sight, and that's where it stayed, dusty and untouched, until now.

I gathered up the scraps of paper and lay back on my bed to read. It was time to remind myself why I had to leave home in the first place.

57

December 15, at 11:00 p.m., the phone rang. It was my brother, Nick, calling from Florida. He had recently joined the Air Force and was stationed in Fort Walton Beach. He had bad news: Daddy had been killed in a car accident earlier that night.

"I just talked to Mama and she asked me to call you," he said. "She's pretty messed up about everything."

He said the funeral was going to be held in Spring Hill. The family had recently moved back there and Daddy had gotten a job teaching government at the high school, as well as coaching the golf and tennis teams. Mama had attained a GED and was in the process of fulfilling a long-time dream of earning a nursing degree. She was now employed part-time at the local hospital as a physical therapist.

Nick had to get off the phone. He said he would call back with the details later. As he was about to hang up, I stopped him. "When Mama told you to call me, did she say my name? Did she tell you to call *Tuesday*?"

"I can't remember..."

"Well, *think*, Nick."

"What difference does it make anyway?"

"It's important to me."

"I remember now. No, no, she didn't. She said your sister, call your sister."

"Thanks Nick. I'll talk to you later."

After I hung up, the first thought to enter my mind was the last conversation I had with Daddy when he had visited me at Aunt Macy's just weeks earlier. Once again he said he was sorry for what he'd allowed Mama to do to me. He told me it was the only thing left in his life he needed to make right, almost as if he knew what was to come. Although he didn't ask, I sensed he wanted me to forgive him then, to say the words. But out of bitterness, I refused to give him what he needed. Now that he was gone, I wished I hadn't let him leave with his guilt that day, forcing him to carry the burden of it with him up until the last tragic moment of his life.

Right before he left, he had told me he loved me, like he did every time we talked, whether over the phone or in person. I always told him back, but the words, shrouded in my anger and pain, often came through as insincere. But I did love him. I'd always loved him and I wanted to tell him like I meant it, but I couldn't. I had never completely given up on him. I was still waiting for him to rescue me, but now I had to face the truth that it was never going to happen. All this regret settled like a rock in the pit of my stomach.

Two days before Daddy's funeral, Aunt Macy and I drove to Spring Hill for the showing. We pulled into the crowded funeral home parking lot, and circled around a few times until we found an empty spot.

I flipped down the sun visor and checked my makeup in the mirror on the back. In the natural light, I saw the little scar that jutted into my upper lip and was suddenly taken back to the day it happened. I shook the memory from my head and fumbled around in my purse until I found some lip gloss. I smeared it on, pressed my lips together to spread it out, fluffed my bangs and got out of the car.

Walking into the funeral home, I could feel Aunt Macy's hand trembling at the base of my back. I had been so wrapped up in my own emotions I'd forgotten she had lost both her mother and her baby brother in a short period of time. I looked at her, beside me, and was struck by how much she'd grown to resemble Grandma Storm now that her hair had turned silver around her temple.

We paused just beyond the threshold. The murmur of condolences filled the room. Through the tears welling in my eyes, I saw a blur of black suits and dark dresses milling around, and the somber faces of Daddy's family and acquaintances. Several young people were there, most of them Daddy's students. He had touched many lives during his years as a teacher and coach. Off in one corner of the room was a group of about six teenage boys in purple letterman jackets—tough jock types—huddled together, crying openly. There were flowers everywhere; the air was thickly perfumed with the smell of them. One of the largest arrangements was done up in purple and gold, the colors of the high school where Daddy taught. It had a satin banner draped across the front, with "Coach" written in glitter.

Daddy's accident made the front page of the local paper. He was described as a well-rounded person and respected long time educator, touted for his sincere depth of interest in how his students developed as individuals. No one ever suspected that a man who gave so much of himself to so many children could betray one of his own.

As Aunt Macy and I approached Daddy's casket, I saw, propped in front, a framed black and white photograph of him when he was a much younger man. The casket was closed because his body had been mangled from the accident and was not fit to be presented to the public. The authorities said he never saw the tractor-trailer rig pull out; he didn't even hit the brakes before he plowed right into the side of the flatbed. The paper stated he had died from severe injuries to the head, but the truth was he'd almost been decapitated.

Most all of my relatives from Daddy's side of the family were there and a few from Mama's. Some of them smiled at me and then darted their eyes away from mine. Others searched out my face as if they wanted to say something. Aunt Barbara was the first one who had the nerve to come up to me.

As she was walking my way, my mind was filing through everything I'd heard Mama say about her over the years: she was plain and big-boned; she never had many dates growing up and she had to go to college to develop her mind because she wasn't pretty. Mama's derogatory remarks were just another example of the insecurity she experienced after her accident, of her trying to make every woman around her less attractive so she would look better. In reality, Aunt Barbara was beautiful, a taller version of Mama.

She embraced me warmly. After salutations, condolences and general niceties she turned the conversation to my childhood, saying she knew Mama didn't treat me "the same as her other kids," and that she was sorry she had allowed it to continue. I understood she needed to unload the guilt she had been carrying around and I tried to focus on what she was saying, but my mind was somewhere else.

"Aunt Barbara, I wish I could tell Daddy that I don't blame him for what Mama did to me. I wish I could tell him how much I love him."

"Oh, honey, he knows, he knows."

"No, you don't understand. I was trying to punish him, to make him suffer..."

"Tuesday, don't. Don't do this to yourself."

Suddenly the sweet smell of flowers made me queasy and I was overcome by the urge to bolt from the room. I excused myself from Aunt Barbara, telling her I was going outside for some fresh air.

On my way out the door, someone touched me on the shoulder. I turned around and saw it was Uncle Max, Daddy's older brother. I hadn't seen him since Grandma Storm's funeral. He lived in Michigan somewhere.

"Tuesday, you mind if I talk with you for a minute?" he asked. "There's something I need to tell you." He took me by the arm and pulled me aside to a private area of the funeral home. "Did you know your dad put away some money for you?"

"No, I didn't."

"It's in a savings account at the bank where I work. He sent me a check several years ago, and asked me to use it to open an account in both your names. Every month he sent what he could manage. It's not a lot of money; your dad wasn't a rich man, but it's enough to get you started in college when the time comes."

"Why did he have an account all the way up in Michigan?"

"He didn't want Rose to know about it. He told me she was having some complications from her accident and she might not understand. Didn't make much sense to me either, but he was my baby brother and it seemed important to him."

"Well, thank you for doing it, Uncle Max, and thanks for letting me know."

"He asked me to make sure you got it if anything ever happened to him. I said I would, but I never imagined he would die before me." He squeezed my hand. "I know it's a hard time for you right now, but I wanted to tell you in person. I'll send you all the information in the mail next week. You're still living at Macy's, right?"

"Yes." I reached up and hugged him around the neck. I had to stand on the tips of my toes, because he was tall like Daddy. "Thank you so much."

"Take care, Tuesday. You'll be hearing from me soon," he said as he walked away.

Outside, I filled my lungs with cold air and tried to process what Uncle Max had just told me.

Aunt Macy came out and joined me. "There you are. Are you okay, sweetie?"

"I'm fine. Aunt Macy, did you know Daddy had been saving money for me?"

"Yes, I did."

"But why?"

"He wanted to help you go to college." She walked around in front of me and took hold of both my arms. "You know, Tuesday, we Storms are pretty good at making lemonade."

"Lemonade?" I asked, puzzled. Then I remembered and grinned. "It's what Grandma used to say—when life gives you lemons, make lemonade."

"That's right! Now, take what you've been through and turn it into something positive."

As soon as we walked back into the funeral home, I saw Mama. She was drifting from person to person, soaking up their sympathy. Her eyes were swollen from crying, her face was flush.

As I had expected, my initial emotion was anger. Then fear of how she might react when she saw me. I was even a little sorry for her, now that Daddy was gone. But what I hadn't expected to feel was the same love and longing for her approval as when I was eight years old.

As always, my three brothers were close by her side. They had been conditioned from an early age to believe her negative treatment of me was because I was bad, the same way I had been conditioned to believe it. I wondered, as I looked at them now, if they had struggled with memories of the horrible things they had seen happen and if these memories had caused them to have conflicting emotions. Or if they had simply chosen to deal with our past the same way I was dealing with it, the way Daddy had dealt with it, by not dealing with it.

Jimmy D. saw me first. He whispered something in Mama's ear and the instant she spotted me, she started walking my way. I wanted to run. Run away from her. Run to her. Frozen, I stood there watching her as she came closer and closer and then stopped in front of me. I tried to read her expression, but her grief was like a mask. Aunt Macy squeezed the back of my arm to show her support.

Why did you come? Go away! I hate you! These were the words that scraped through my head like fingernails across a chalkboard. But in my ear I heard a soft sweet voice. "Ladybug, I'm glad you're here." I felt her arms around me. "I'm glad you're here," she whispered again, and I was relieved when she did because I thought I had imagined it the first time.

In an instant, I was eight years old again and in my mama's arms. My knees buckled, and I could feel Aunt Macy holding me up.

Two days later, Aunt Macy and I came back to Spring Hill for Daddy's funeral. Mama sat beside me during the service. Once, she reached for my hand. Afterward we held each other again, but this time it felt obligatory. Then she went back to her house in Spring Hill and I went home with Aunt Macy.

A week later, when I got in from school, I found a package on the front porch addressed simply to Ladybug. I opened it and inside found a gold bangle bracelet with delicate flower etchings. Immediately I recognized it as the one Jerry Stevens had given me for Christmas in seventh grade. No note of explanation was attached, no return address. But then, there was no need for either one.

Later on that night, I gathered up the nerve to call her, but she didn't answer the phone. In the days and weeks to follow, I tried to reach her many more times, with no luck. Eventually I gave up and got on with my life.

58

On my seventeenth birthday, Aunt Macy and I ate lunch at Shoney's, and then went back to the house for my traditional German chocolate cake.

Aunt Macy always made a big deal out of my birthday, even though it was only the two of us. Every year, she put the exact number of candles as my age on the cake, lit them and sang "Happy Birthday to You" all the way through. Then she insisted I blow out the candles in one breath and make a wish. It was all so corny and I loved every minute of it.

"You ready for cake?" she asked, taking the candles out one at a time and laying them on the counter.

With a poker face, I answered, "No, I think I'll eat the napkins this year."

She eyed me for a second and then we both laughed.

We could now joke about my eating paper because it was no longer a problem. Since the doctor had put me on iron supplements, my craving had diminished to where it wasn't in my face every day, but rather lurking, quietly below the surface of my conscious. Dr Jernigan told me I was fortunate, because some people always have pica; but in my case, it was due to a mineral deficiency from poor nutrition and therefore treatable.

"I am so proud of you," said Aunt Macy, as she cut a huge wedge from the cake and placed it on the pink paper plate in front of me. "I think you made a sensible decision about what to do with the money your daddy left you."

It was a decision that came to me without much effort on my part. In the months after Daddy's death, I began to sense a stronger presence of the lonely, frightened child within me, the little girl who no one had loved enough to help. Her doleful face stared back at me from every reflective surface. At night, she crouched at the foot of my bed crying, and when I surrendered to sleep, she slipped in through the back door of my mind.

I didn't know how to comfort her, how to repair the damage that had been done. I was afraid I would only fail her again. But I didn't want to be like the others who had ignored her for all those years and kept her hidden, pretending as if she didn't exist.

I started paying more attention to the children around me, wondering if there might be others who were suffering in the same way I had. Whenever I saw a despondent expression in the eyes of a young girl on the street, I couldn't help but think she might be concealing something, protecting someone she loved, as I had. Every time I passed a house that reminded me of the one I grew up in on Maplewood Drive, I wondered if it harbored secrets, if there could be a hopeless, little someone inside crying out to deaf ears.

I knew I couldn't go back in time and save the child I once was, but I had the power to do the next best thing and that was to try to help others like her. I decided when I graduated from high school, I would take the money Daddy had put aside for me and enroll in Franklin Community College, near Nashville, in the associate's degree program in social services.

"Do you think it's what Daddy would have wanted me to do?" I asked Aunt Macy.

"It's *exactly* what your daddy would've wanted."

Confident I was headed in the right direction, I smiled wide and dug into my cake.

About two o'clock that afternoon, I was getting dressed to go to the movies with some friends when the phone rang.

"I'll get it," I hollered out to Aunt Macy. I was sure it was one of my friends calling to say she was running late.

"Hello," I said into the phone.

"Happy birthday, Ladybug!" came a gleeful voice from the other end. It had been nearly seven months since I'd last seen Mama at Daddy's funeral, and I hadn't spoken to her since.

"Thanks, Mama," I said.

"I can't believe you're seventeen years old!" she rattled on. "It seems like only yesterday we were celebrating your eighth birthday! Do you remember the red dotted sun-suit I gave you that year?"

"Yeah, I remember, that's why you started calling me Ladybug."

"You know, Ladybug, I got you a little something for your birthday and I made your favorite, German chocolate cake. I was wondering if you and Macy might like to come over tonight and help me and the boys eat it."

I didn't even have to think about it. I would call my friends and tell them something more important had come up. "Sure, if it's okay with Aunt Macy."

When we arrived at Mama's house in Spring Hill, Jimmy D., now almost fifteen, and Ryan, six, met us at the door. It felt awkward being around Ryan, because I never had the chance to get to know him before I left home. But it didn't take long for Jimmy D. and me to pick right back up where we had left off that morning at the kitchen table before everything changed.

We all sat in the living room and ate our cake and ice cream and talked about everyday subjects—normal family things like Aunt Macy's tomato plants and Jimmy D.'s new girlfriend. Everything was fine with Mama and me, as long as I acted like nothing bad had ever happened between us.

After we finished eating, I opened the present Mama had been exploding to give me since I walked through the door, a spaghetti-strap sundress—red with black polka dots.

"I couldn't resist," she said. Then she threw her head back and laughed in the same carefree way she had before her accident. In that instant, I saw a snapshot of who she once was. It was but a fleeting image—I blinked and it was gone—but it was enough to let me know that behind the fog in her mind that protected her, my mama was still in there somewhere.

In the car, on the way back home, I was bubbly with excitement, talking miles a minute, recounting the night and how much fun it had been.

"Don't get your hopes up too high, missy," Aunt Macy warned. And I knew she was right.

59

Two years went by quickly. Mama stayed busy with the boys and her new job as a nurse, and I threw myself into my schoolwork, but we tried to keep in touch as best we could. I called her whenever I got the chance, and once in a while, she even answered the phone. There was no pattern to when she contacted me. Sometimes I would hear from her every day for weeks in a row, and then there would be a stretch of time when weeks would pass in between her calls. But she made sure we got together on my eighteenth and nineteenth birthdays.

On the Memorial Day before I turned twenty, she called to ask if I would meet her at the cemetery in Spring Hill, where Daddy and Audrey were buried. "I'm not going to bring the boys this time," she said on the phone. "I want it to be just us girls."

I arrived at the cemetery first and waited until Mama drove up. As soon as she parked her car, she got out and ran to greet me. She had on a tailored navy pantsuit and pumps to match. She was letting her hair go back to its natural color. I noticed her strawberry blond waves were streaked with a little gray. "So good to see you, Ladybug!" she squealed. She still hadn't brought herself to call me by my name. To her, I was Ladybug, the eight-year-old girl who'd never had anything bad happen to her.

We chatted for a while, catching up on each other's lives and then walked to the graves together. She cleared the debris from the gravesites and I held the flowers she'd brought. For Audrey, we had her favorite red tulips and for Daddy, fuzzy pink mimosa blooms. He always loved them. Every spring he would cut a few limbs from the tree in the backyard of our house on Maplewood and make a huge bouquet for the kitchen table.

Mama knelt beside Daddy's headstone and brushed the dirt from the words *Beloved Husband and Father*. She did the same for Audrey's, which read *Angel Unaware*.

"Your daddy would be so happy to know we're here together, wouldn't he?" she said, taking the tulips from me and placing them in the vase on Audrey's grave.

"Yes, he would, Mama, very happy."

Daddy had once told me that if I wanted to have a future with Mama I might have to let go of the past. I now knew what he had meant by that. Whether it was by her choosing, or her body's way of protecting her, everything she'd done to me in the five years after her accident had simply vanished from her memory. I, however, had not been able to forget. But I was slowly learning to pluck the flowers of my past from the weeds and place them in the window of my mind where I could see them first.

Mama turned around and extended her hand. "Give me those mimosa branches, would you, Ladybug?"

She looked up at me with soft eyes that held no trace of the cruel woman she'd once been. But even so, in those eyes I saw only shadows of the person she was before her accident.

And although I was suddenly saddened when I realized that the mother I'd idolized as a child may never fully return, I knew all was not lost. I still had this:

It's a squint-eye sunny day in July, my eighth birthday. I tie together the ends of the dandelion necklace I just finished making and place it around Mama's neck.

"For me?" she says, as if she didn't know.

"Yep," I answer proudly. "I made it for you."

"It's stunning!" she says, all dramatic, like a movie star.

"I love you, Mama."

She smiles. "Love you more, Tuesday."

Made in the USA
Middletown, DE
13 July 2021